Steve Wraith

Steve Wraith is always spinning ɪ probably best know for being ʟʜᴇ ᴇᴅɪʟᴏɪ ᴏɪ ʀɪayers ɪnc Magazine. The former Newcastle United Fans Liaison Officer is slowly creeping towards his 40th year on planet earth and still doesn't know what he wants to be when he grows up.

He lives at the bottom of a hill and is married with 1 bairn and another on the way and a black cat with a white paw.

Andy Singe Thompson

The debut book from Singe, in his profession he's an arboriculturalist (does stuff with trees), he's a life long Newcastle United fan and one time Grange Villa centre forward/substitute. More often than not he dabbles in photography and submits articles to Players Inc magazine.

Singe lives on top of a hill and is married with 2 bairns, a ferret, some chickens and not forgetting his little black dog with a white paw.

4

FOREWORD

by Malcolm Macdonald

It won't be lost on the remaining Championship clubs that two of the relegated Premier League sides have not only gone straight back up, but have done it at pretty much of a canter.

Newcastle United and West Bromwich Albion set about each other on the opening day of the season

in such exciting fashion their standards generally were never going to be matched by the second tier also rans.

So what made these two teams so much better than the rest? Simply they stuck to the basics of the game and were better at them than all of their opponents. What are these basics that are so important then?

Quitre simply it is encompassed in three words. Control and pass. Say those three words and then do it. But, and this is the important bit, can you do it as quickly as you say it?

Newcastle United controlled the ball quicker than anybody else, that meant they could pass it quicker than the rest and in doing so maintained accuracy.

That in turn took them very quickly from one end of the pitch to the other and they turned the phrase to control and shoot, and stayed equally accurate in that skill as they did with their passing.

Look at any league table at any level of the game of football. Whichever club is at the top they have controlled the ball better, they passed more accurately and their shooting was more on target.

Control, pass and shoot are the three simple basics of the game. Treasure them, do them well and they in turn will do you well like they did Newcastle United this promotion season.

INTRODUCTION

NEWCASTLE UNITED FOOTBALL CLUB
Formed 1882

Honours

1905 – Division One Winners
1907 – Division One Winners
1909 – Division One Winners
1910 – FA Cup Winners
1924 – FA Cup Winners
1927 – Division One Winners
1932 – FA Cup Winners
1951 – FA Cup Winners
1952 – FA Cup Winners
1955 – FA Cup Winners
1965 – Division Two Winners
1969 – Fairs Cup Winners
1993 – Division One (2nd Div) Winners

Newcastle United a club steeped in tradition and heritage, a club based on under achieving and impatience, corruption and greed. A club with a worldwide fan base who constantly fail to provide. The 2008/2009 season witnessed the demise of a club in farcical and highly embarrassing circumstances. A not to popular portly bloke from down south running the show like some sort of self destroying buffoon, Keegan sacked/pushed/quit for not wanting to sign a player off YouTube. Coach Chris Hughton takes temporary charge then the appointment of a medically unfit, tourette's suffering mad Irishman in the form of Joe Kinnear who's been out of football for 83 years. Kinnear swears a lot then has a heart attack, Hughton gets the job back. April fool's day has the appointment of The Lion of Gosforth Alan Shearer as the 4th manager of the season as a last role of the dice for survival. The last day of the campaign away to Aston Villa sees us needing only a point to stay up. Newcastle lose the 4 team battle for the last relegation place which ends our proud 16 year stay in the Premier League at the expense of Hull fucking City. The nation goes wild with over sensationalist media headlines at our demise Sunderland treat the occasion as if they had won the league.

It now seems everybody's 'favourite 2nd team' are a laughing stock as we prepare for life in the wilderness of the Fizzy Pop League with the big wage earning badly performing waste of space footballers who got us into this mess jumping ship like drowning rats. An owner who doesn't want us, a club for sale that apparently nobody wants to buy, no money, no team, no manager, no passion, no drive, no commitment and no fans

Can promotion be gained to the promised land of the Premier League first time around?

GRANGE VILLA WMC FOOTBALL CLUB
Formed 1982

Honours
1998 – Stanley Sunday League Div 2 Winners
2002 – Richardson Cup Winners
2002 – Bev Hagget Cup Winners

Grange Villa is a typical former North Eastern mining village. It suffers from the effects that all abandoned industrial community's suffer, anti social problems, petty crime, gangs of kids roaming the streets, substance misuse and vandalism. It's socially acceptable for women to go down the corner shop in their pyjamas at 11.30am on a Thursday.

The one glimmer of comfort is the slimming club and the over 60's coffee morning at the local community centre.

There is also a football team.....

Grange Villa WMC.FC are a Sunday morning football side formed way back in the depth of 1982, they currently play in the Gateshead and District 1st Division.

The management of the team is made up by secretary Singe (who was voted as having the best shoes on a club trip to Thirsk Races one year). Assistant Manager Podge a former Stanley League player of the year. Clak a rude, sarcastic man who had both leg's implanted with titanium kneecaps. And the main drive behind the team is the long standing manager Sharpey who's given up countless thousand Friday night's to sell domino cards in Grange Villa Club to finance the team. The four of them have a combined time of 35 years devotion to The Villa football team.

So it's a sound managerial team, financially stable, 36 decent footballer's (school teachers, policemen and local councillors amongst them) signed on for the 2009/2010 season the future looks dam pretty.

One slight snag is we never win fuck all. In 27 years of Sunday Morning football we have the success of 2 cups and 1 now defunct Stanley and District Sunday League 2nd Division championship under our belts. A small return for the countless hours of unseen, time consuming and un-thanking hard work that goes on.

Of course last season yet again the Villa made an utter hash of their challenge for promotion. After being top for long spells of the season they finish a massively disappointing 8th place after a loss of form. The biggest culprit was Star turn DC having an ice cream eating relapse as well as Maradona Davidson catching thrush from Thunder Mitchell's toilet seat.

Can promotion be gained to the promised land of the Premier League this time around?

AUGUST

So this is the fizzy pop league?

This season already promises to be as mad as last with Joe Kinnear ironically appearing at the launch of a game called 'Championship Manager' and claiming that he has been offered a two year contract at St James. Nowt would surprise me like. He has to wait until the doctor gives him the go ahead though! Men in white coats more like. Meanwhile talks of another takeover bid surface with Geordie saviour and local entrepreneur Barry Moat raising his ginger head above the parapet. It sounds too good to be true to be honest and I swear that I've seen this bloke at the match with Mike Ashley and Co. His bid is as likely as mine at this stage. He needs the £100 million pounds first up then needs to guarantee that he can manage the clubs overdraft. Further rumours surfacing that Ashley may sell to hedge fund investors in the smoke. As each day, week, month goes by I really feel that Mike Ashley and Co. are going to be with us for a while to come. Watch this space.

With the clock ticking down to the new season, Steven Taylor decides to open his heart to the 'Ronnie Gill' and shows that all in the garden behind the scenes is not as rosy as Chris Hughton would have us believe. "I've read every week that Alan Shearer is going to be named manager, then Joe Kinnear is going to get the job, then Kevin Keegan and then Alan again. I don't get it. It's a joke. The players are very frustrated because all we want to do is have a manager and a bit of stability. Barton kicks off in training and hoys a wobbler with Chris Hughton. Glad to see the Scouser is ready for the battle that is the Championship! Habib Beye departs for Aston Villa for a paltry £2million. I'm just so glad he didn't join the Makems which his agent tells me was a real possibility!

So here we are a balmy summer's day at the Hawthorns. A Premiership fixture in the division below and a sign of things to come with a 5:30pm kick off on the telly. Don't forget folks this club is of no interest to anybody and even more so now that we have been relegated. Already 5 games swapped to ludicrous kick off times because of Sky and BBC. The minute's applause for Sir Bobby Robson is the best I have ever experienced. It was fitting that two sides he served so well should face each other. The game itself is a tight affair and we come away with a point after a 1-1 draw with Tim Krul winning the plaudits in goal after replacing Steve Harper after Shola Ameobi took it upon himself to belt Harper in the head instead of clearing the ball. Duff grabs what could turn out to be an important goal, whichever end of the table we find ourselves at come May. Needless to say no sign of Joey Barton confirming the rumours that our Scouse cobble champion has indeed fell out with the manager all be it caretaker once again.

The rumour mill is in overdrive again with David O'Leary spotted in Gills Fish and Chip emporium in Felling. He apparently will land the manager's job and not a large haddock and chips paper in the near future. That means that Mike Ashley and Co. are no longer interested in Alan Shearer after saying that his appointment was the 'best decision' they had ever made. If I were Alan I'd sit tight until the new owner comes in. Ok I know we may all be governed by Daleks by then, but is our former Number Nine legend really going to get a fair crack of the whip with this lot? I doubt it.

Another day, another departure and this time it's our current top scorer Damien 'yet to reach his potential' Duff who is off to pastures new. Fulham the unlucky club who will have to fork out this duffers wages. Having said that we are probably paying his wages for the next five years or something daft like that. You never know with this lot. Still it's another £4 million in Mike Ashley and Co.'s sky rocket. Does all this cash come off the £100 million asking price I wonder? With transfer deadline edging ever closer more players are linked with the exit door. Steven Taylor Everton, Jonas Gutierrez with Olympiakos, Alan Smith anybody in the Premiership. Get the feeling I may have to start taking my size 12 rugby boots complete with steel toe caps to St James in the coming weeks. Stop the press! We have a new arrival at the club. Danny Simpson. A defender from Manchester United has arrived on loan. I hate that factor alone. A feeder club for the club everyone loves to hate. Hope he's better than that forward we had off them a while back.

I've decided to stop buying newspapers! This takeover twaddle is boiling my piss. There is a different story week in week out and I really do believe that Mike Ashley and Co. are here for the long run. The bloke has the skin of a rhino and his presence at our second game of the season a 3-0 romp at home to Reading had us all in good voice. 'Get out of our club, get out of our club, you fat greedy cockney bastard, get out of our club'. Not sure who that was directed at but it rang out loud and proud from the impressive gate bordering on 37,000. Not bad for a fizzy pop league team that nobody has any interest in. The team are really buzzing and showing the fight that was sadly lacking at the back end of last season. A return for Barton, although you would never have known as he was completely ineffective. Shola, often the butt of jokes and terrace jibes can hold his head up high after today's performance. A hat-trick to shut his critics up, including my

13

brother Rob who has developed a whince every time he gets the ball. Shola has found his level. I'm sure Rob will grow to love our number one striker and cure his whince to boot. Just hope Manchester City aren't considering tabling a bid for him. In truth Reading were awful, and it was nice to watch our lads play some half decent football for once.

I've managed to stop buying a paper for two days now (it's harder than giving up tabs! So I've been told.) but had some chips from Gills Emporium in Felling and saw that there was another potential bidder in for Newcastle. Agggghhhhhh!!!! I cannot get away from it man. The thing about the Fizzy Pop League is that the games come thick and fast which could be a real problem with the size of our squad. Sheffield Wednesday in town today and it's like friends reunited. I remember the 83-84 promotion year (my first season) and we were neck and neck with this lot all the way. The rivalry is still as strong as ever. They bring a big squad up and our gate is verging on 44,000. Not bad for a fizzy pop league team that nobody has any interest in. Interestingly enough we have more at our ground for this fixture than Sunderland for their game against Chelsea. You've got Steve Cram as a celebrity fan! Sunderland's' a massive club!

I get home to see 'sickening' images on my television screen. No not a re-run of the '73 Cup Final but Prospective buyer Barry Moat and Mike Ashley and Co. sitting side by side. This whole thing stinks man. I'm telling you now this is a con from start to finish. The latest rumour is that Moat can't even afford the club, and if he can raise the cash then he can't afford to spend on players. Utterly pointless. Unlike our team though. Chris Hughton's black and white army (did I really write that?) are top of the league and unbeaten. Another Ameobi strike earns us a 1-0 win. It can't last can it?

Just caught a bit of Sky Sports. Didn't expect to be on there as much this season with us being in the fizzy pop league we aren't important. Heard Graham Roberts chuntering on about taking the club over. He's apparently representing the Fans 410 Group??? First I've heard of it or the rest of the lads as I quickly text round all and sundry. The idea is to create a Barcelona type model where the fans own/run the club. It will never work. The last thing we need is another ex-Chelsea player walking around the corridors of power at our club. Look what happened with the Dennis Wise man. Roberts claims he will be meeting the chairman. Now we know he is lying. Nobody can get hold of Mike Ashley and Co. ever!

London doesn't hold many happy football memories for me if I'm honest. However Selhurst Park does. I saw the FA Cup trophy here for the first time in 1989. I was on a family holiday in London and was invited to watch Wimbledon who were playing their home games here at the time parade the cup to the fans. It was a carnival atmosphere. At 4:45 the Dons fans were looking to drown their sorrows after a 5-2 drubbing. I was also here for the win in 1994 when Peter Beardsley scored a cracker with seconds remaining. Halcyon days indeed. The way the team set about the task today spoke volumes about the squad's determination to buckle down and get the job done first time around. Although I have to admit that I'd rather have this kind of game week in week out, do I really want to go back to the Premiership and be part of the boring middle tier brigade playing for nothing, or be down at the bottom clinging for dear life facing teams who want to bore you to death by playing for a draw. At least in the Fizzy Pop League teams play to win. Goals from Kevin Nolan and Ryan Taylor sealed a 2-0 win and that means that Taylor only owes us one more and we can forgive him for those free-kicks he curled past us at the JJB.

It beggars belief really. Our chairman/chief executive/ henchman/patsy (delete where applicable) Derek Llambias has allegedly lost a bet with Mike Ashley and Co. and has had to pay a forfeit by streaking naked across the pitch. As you would predict at our club he did it with an uninvited audience of corporate guests who he had thought had left the ground! With this lot it's a surprise they didn't wait until a few journalists were pitch side complete with cameras. Idiot. My mate Alan Payne who sits in front of me at the match tells me that it didn't make front page for a change. I wouldn't know I don't read papers any more. Just as well as he also tells me that Steven Taylor has now been linked with Aston Villa. Tayls reckons he is being pushed out of the club. Wouldn't surprise me. We are running out of saleable assets. I really hope he stays. For me he is the difference between an automatic slot and the play-offs come May.

I don't know where you lot stand on this but I'm a great believer that you make your own luck in this game. I've just heard that Alan Smith (our new skipper) is growing a beard until our first defeat. It's all part of the new 'spirit' in the dressing room which sees the players select tracks for the stereo in the changers and the like. I don't want our lads turning out like ZZ Top, which is likely after witnessing the calibre of teams we are yet to face after watching BBC's excellent Fizzy Pop League coverage.

The Fizzy Lager Cup is up next and has never been a favourite of mine, or previous United teams for that matter as we always seem to dip out at the first or second hurdle, which is infuriating as teams such us Leicester, Oxford, and QPR have at least graced Wembley in its Final. Chris Hughton was obviously in two minds with his team selection. His line up was full of bairns but his bench was full of match winners. The dilemma Hughton faced was does he want to be in the Cup or not? For me winning breeds confidence and you should want to win every competition you enter. If you don't what's the bloody point? Ok I know we have the smallest squad in our history, but surely we are due an injury free season? Yeah ok your right who am I kidding! The game itself was the proverbial seven goal thriller with Guthrie opening proceedings with a screamer and then the Gallowgate being silenced by Lee Clarks' Huddersfield Town roaring into a 3-1 lead. (This is sounding more like an Alan Oliver match report!) After a bit of teacup throwing by Hughton and hairdryering by Calderwood, Shola ambled on for Butt who looked knackered and he changed the game. Geremi reduced the deficit with a neat finish and 'Shola The Goala' despatched a deserved penalty to draw us level. With the game on a knife edge and a place in the last 32 beckoning cometh the hour cometh the man...and Kevin Nolan was that man with a one yard tap in my granny would be proud of after some great work by the provider, yes you've guessed it, Shola. Tell me ma me ma and all that. Move over Lee Ryder! Joking aside this game really showed our lack of strength in depth should our inevitable injury list appear on the horizon. Pointless informing Mike Ashley and Co. of this of course as with everything else it will fall on deaf ears.

Ok I have to come clean here. Myself imposed ban on newspapers is over. I had to give in to the shakes, the hallucinations and the fact that with countless newsagents closing up and down the country in these times of recession I just couldn't bear the guilt if my local paper pusher were to go the same way! Guess what the first story I read is! Yes you've guessed it a 'new' takeover bidder. This time it's an American consortium headed by Geoff Sheard. No sorry he says he's not heading it he's the middle man. Hold on weren't all these prospective buyers supposed to keep it to themselves until the deal was done. Another load of crap. Meanwhile Barry Moat continues his wonderful audition for the part of the Invisible Man. You have got the part Baz!

More rumours circulating about Tayls leaving for Everton and now Andy Carroll being linked with West Ham. Kevin Nolan Bolton, Alan Smith Everton and Bolton the list is endless. Most of the nationals have it in for us so have decided to bin them and stick with the 'Ronnie Gill.' At least they are on our side. Aren't they? After my failed attempt at boycotting newspapers I'm going to ban myself from watching transfer deadline day on Sky Sports News. Is it just me or are they starting that bloody countdown clock at the close of the last window. Mike Ashley and Co. have made the whole window thing a bit of a non-event for us since they took over so don't expect any fireworks or ticker tape signings. We head into the Indian summer with another three points against Leicester at home with another 38,000 gate at Gallowgate. Guthrie grabbing the winner after good work by Nile Ranger. Not quite singing we are top of the league yet, but we are all starting to believe a little more. Why I don't know 'cos we all know that things will unravel and go to shit as they inevitably do. Shola out injured. Talk is of a two month lay-off. See what did I tell you. Hats off to Leicester's fans for that old retro classic 'Your shit ahhhhhhh' chant at Harpers' kicks.

I got a call today from a guy in London asking if I'll front a new web talk in focussing on Newcastle United. I'm no Supermac but I've agreed to give it a go.

'Toon Talk' is launched and big thanks to all the lads who rang in tonight. A few hiccups but all in all it went well. Show available on ITunes if you're interested!

Chris Hughton named as Manager Of The Month and Shola player of the month. Well done lads!

Washington Steps
Kick off

The league AGM came and went during the summer and was to be honest was a bloody farce.

The night before Britain's Toughest Villages had been re-shown on Sky TV for the 118th time let us not forget that the program was first aired in 2004 and to us civilized, sophisticated people this is slightly old news now. If the daft old twats in the club wanted to show themselves up on Sky by talking about how hard they are and how the 'Phantom Leek Slasher' eats children let them, nothing at all to do with us footballers.

So a lot of whoo harr was undoubtedly created at the AGM about our appearance on the box by those who watched it. The Travellers Rest said they thought they were tougher than us and The Villa was too far away from Gateshead to actually be able to play in the league. Podge did offer the option of them stepping up to the plate and making an official challenge to the 'hard' title. This challenge was unfortunately turned down due to them not having any socks other than white Terry Towel ones. You know the ones you buy from the Quayside Market on a Sunday a zillion pairs for a quid. As for the jibe about us being too far away from Gateshead I can only assume there ASBO's and early release prison tags prevent them from travelling the 8 miles from Gateshead to Grange Villa.

For some reason they don't like us very much this lot.

Not to be out done North Biddick from the Premier League who we have never even played in our 28 year history also thought they could have a cheap shot at us about sheep. Anybody with any education would know that Grange Villa is in fact a former mining village. Somebody representing North Biddick should know this as North Biddick is the home of The Durham Mining Museum.

For the record the only farm in Grange Villa is a dairy farm and does not stock any sheep at all.

The summer also had the return of Hardy moving back to us from The Westwood (where he never even got a game). Hardy as we all know is a Villa lad and something of a prankster, as well as journeyman footballer. Others including me like to call him a fucking nuisance, he's most famous for eating shit from a pair of Flares night club knickers one Sunday morning.

So the 2009/2010 season started with me nicking a plum from manager Sharpy's fruit bowl then arriving at the nuclear bunker changing room that Hood's Nan built over the summer to find Hardy proudly showing of a 50p piece.

It was a funny metallic brown colour. Apparently he swallowed it last week after training then retrieved it a couple of days later. Not only happy with showing this off he actually swallowed the thing again! It's going to be a long, long season.

Mr Wine and Cheese Clues had been on kit wash duty due to Sharpey being away and the little tinker thought it would be funny to swap the Villa strip's for a set of 1970's kid's strips. Sharpey failed to see the funny side of it and took a massive strop; he swore then spat on the floor. I won't report on the fact that he also kicked seven bells out of the changing room door or Hoods Nan might get mad. To go along with the gag all the lads tried to change into the 70's kit. The fat lads amongst us did look rather fetching in there ultra tight bairns tops.

The game was barely 10mins old when Hardy managed to dislocate his shoulder. He spent a while wriggling around the pitch and hyper active Sharpey took his 2nd strop of the day as nobody could magic a bandage out of fresh air. As per usual the Villa kit man had forgotten the first aid box!

A paramedic turned up gave Hardy gas and air but unfortunately couldn't take the poor lad to hospital due to his oversized and ample belly. A second ambulance was then duly dispatched to rescue him. Any x-ray he might have will obviously show up a 50p coin in his belly.

So much for our new super star signing, we all wish him a quick recovery.

Talking of injury's, the injured Tinhead spent all morning kicking an American football around the Villa with the equally injured Stupid Ben. They were also told off for trying to climb a garden fence to recover the above mentioned stray American football by neighbour Bone Crusher Bob.

Following on from Hardy's injury Marshall had to play centre forward The Villa Ultras then promptly christened him Slug Marshall due to his pace or the complete lack of it.

Villa Ultra Goat Mitchell also announced that he won't smoke roly tabs anymore this is not for smoke related health reason but for the fact that smoking cigarettes can give you Aids. All smokers should be aware of this. Not sure why the government hasn't put a health warning on the side of the packet.

21

Podge and DC had a big bitch fight during the game apparently DC is not the super star he thinks he is. He was also caught off-side 400 times during the match. If we get as many points as he's caught off-side we should piss the league.....easy!

Today's two subs Police constable Hutchy made his return back to the side from a long absence and it took him less than 12 seconds before his famous war cry of 'Man, Fuck' was heard. The other sub was former Villa Ultra Young Pyle making his official Villa debut he did okay but it was noted in some circles that he can't grow rhubarb as good as his Dad, Old Pyle.

Crumb Two Cans turned up stinking of drink and possibly illegal narcotics asking if he can sign on for the season. Sharpey made a sharp exit and left him talking to Singe where he was informed that Crumb Two cans was a good player and worthy of a game. He then announced that 'it's not all about tricks it's all about speed' I'm sure he'd had a gram of speed before he turned up to pester the life out of me.

The result was a hard fought but deserved 2.1 victory and a decent opening game of the season for The Villa.

Travellers Rest
Wellington Boots

We made our annual trip to Wrekington to play The Travellers Rest. Funny how we always get them on a Tuesday night the 2nd game of the season. At least we didn't have that referee who has the Newcastle Falcons badge bleached into the back of his hair as in all fairness he's not too good and rumoured to actually drink in The Travellers bar

It's funny how they also like to kick the shit out of us every year.

The difference between this year and last was that it was sunny, oh and this year we had 17 ton of cut grass scattered around the pitch.

Sharpey was again missing from the side lines due to his West Yorkshire hole digging fetish. Ever since Knick Knack Knob Jimmy D took the huff last season Sharpey has picked up this awful habit of spitting on the floor when he gets angry, don't know what or why he does this for. But we did have a peaceful evening tonight without him and no need for umbrellas or waterproof coats.

The Villa side was an odd miss match hobbled together in a rush. Tuesday night games are a right nuisance with lads working etc. We were one step away from stopping random people in the street and asking if they fancied a game at one point. Even Veterans Singe and Clak got a run out at the end.

The match itself was a hard fought 2.0 victory against a decent side. And fair play to The Travellers as they appear to have cut out the gnarly, mad man attitude they seem to have against us and got on and played some canny football as well.

Tinhead could possibly be as numb as a winter's day in Stanley but well done to him for forgetting his injury and putting his boots on and helping out when we were short. He did however get rather excited about a gaggle of female joggers running past the pitch. Poor lad obviously doesn't get out much.

The best crack of the night came from Adam Marshall who turned up to watch the lads with his mate Dirty Den. Adam of course is Slug Marshall's brother and he spilled the beans on Slug, who apparently is still scared of the dark and when he needs a wee wee in the night he pisses in an old

Wellington boot in the corner of his bedroom. He also claimed that Slug ran away from home when he was little and lasted just under an hour. He returned home as he was hungry. This explains a hell of a lot.

Some good and bad news on the injury front, Hardy could be back fit within a month after his dislocated shoulder on Sunday. He was seen at work with his arm in a sling shouting obscenities out of a window at the council cutting the grass.

Stupid Ben on the other hand could be out longer as Goat Mitchell (on his birthday) turned up with his stupid American Football. Let's just say Ben fell over.

Sunday and we travel back to Moss Heaps to take on Greencroft

Greencroft
Free drink and Administration errors
My week with The Villa started on Thursday when I was contacted by the league regarding an administration irregularity. Obviously for legal reasons I can't comment further at this moment in time but let's just say I wish Chris Clues had spent more time at pre-season training other than hosting wine and cheese party's. The story will be unravelled in the forthcoming weeks.

Better news was made on Friday night at Tiger Tiger in Newcastle as I was a guest of Steve Wraith and Players Inc Magazine. Let's just say I did the Villa proud in the amount of free alcohol I managed to consume. Tony from the Thomas Wilson was gob smacked when I ordered Crayfish and Avocado for my starter. He said people from The Villa haven't even heard of avocado and I only ordered it sound posh and to fit in.

I had to leave the party early to catch the last train to Scotland (with as much free drink as I could carry) where I was appearing in the Edinburgh Fringe Festival. Everybody knows I have a big one.

Fringe that is.

So my Sunday actually started at 7am as I left bonny Scotland to travel back down the A1 to Moss Heaps as Greencroft entertained the Villa. Now that's dedication to the cause.

To be honest it was a quiet day on the side lines as most of the Ultras are in Magaluf throwing berries and American footballs at tourists. The Ultras are so famous there not actually famous at all.

DC admitted he'd spent the week learning the offside rule on the internet after his 17th decision against him last Sunday. I just hope he looked up football and not ice hockey.

The result was a hard fought but disappointing 1.0 defeat against a strong and organised Greencroft side. The highlight of the day was The Greencroft's Max Branning look-alike calling Sharpey a 'fucking tramp' if only language like this was used in Eastenders

Max Branning obviously doesn't know that Sharpey lives in the affluent Thornton's Close part of Pelton. Sharpey is so posh he even has a drive as well as a garage. (No car mind).

Slug Marshall did manage to get involved in a handbag throwing; hissy fit in the last minute of the game to be fair to him it's his first one of the season.

Highwayman
Awful

The night started with a request from the Highwayman's secretary to borrow a keeper shirt due to the clash in colour.

25

They had to tape over the C.J.D Haulage sponsorship logo due to T.V rights as our games are always on the box. The big metal fences around the pitch from last season had been moved and replaced with a big hole. Not sure what sort of development is going on here.

We then found ourselves a goal down after 60 seconds due to an error from P.C Hutchinson. Mind you he's looking more Kebabcop then Robocop these days.

Former Villa Ultra Hend turned up to watch and said the reason for his absence from the side lines over the last few games was that he'd become the first person to pogo stick his way to the North Pole unaided. Well done to him on this mean feat.

Slug Marshall equalised with a 'BOOSH' type goal. This one was a shin roller from 1 yard out. This goal made up for his crinkled, un-ironed Villa training top that he turned up in. This man is a local councillor as well.

Bloody politicians.

Slug's goal got the Highwayman's designated linesman a bright shade of purple with anger. He was so purple it looked like he'd had a fortnight in Turkey drinking nothing other than neat Vimto.

Unfortunately Slug's goal was as good as it got as we crashed to an embarrassing and well deserved 6.2 twating. Only Skipper Brown put in a shift of note. There was to be no highway robbery tonight as basically we were shit.

Half time was spent with the lads again squabbling on amongst themselves like a bunch of hissy girls, this has to stop.

Chrisy P (best looking lad at the Villa) told me before the game he used to play centre forward for Scotland. Chrisy P then managed to squander a simple chance when one on one with the keeper.

Believe it or not but Ally McCoist used to play football for Sunderland.

He was better on A Question of Sport. Chrisy P is better at left back.

End of story.

Dirty Den admitted tonight that he actually doesn't sell cars for a living his job is to grind off engine serial numbers with a Stihl Saw.

The Villa have a free week next Sunday as the pitch is getting used for the 15th annual Grange Villa Carnival. Daryl Tottle has arranged an NUFC v SAFC cricket game from the oldies in the club.

SEPTEMBER

A European trip!

The window slams shut and we have given Peter Loverkrands a three year deal after sending him packing with a letter at the end of last term. He must be the first person to squeeze money out of Mike Ashley and Co. since they got here, because he must have had them over the proverbial barrel, as it's taken some time to get him back through the door. Let's hope he lives up to expectations as he looked the best of a bad bunch last season. Total spends then? Nowt. Cheers Mike Ashley and Co. At least Tayls clung on in the player cull and we seem to have some cloggers and grafters who can at least keep us in this division. Oh apparently Xisco has gone to Racing Santander on a season loan. God help them.

Still no movement on the sale front. Next doors house that is. Might as well keep you updated on that because it's got more chance of going through than the sale of the club. Kevin Keegan v Newcastle United court case is looming nearer although nobody seems to know when it is. The London based media are revelling in all of this crap and would love to see us cover ourselves in the brown sticky stuff on and off the pitch so that we can flog a few more red tops. I think we all know 'Special K' will handle his end with dignity. It will be Mike Ashley and Co. and 'Dirty' Dennis Wise who will be shown up for what they are. Some of the message boards lately have fans split on who is to blame? These people siding against 'Wor Kev' must have a slate loose or as I expect are 'Makems' from cherry knowles. Kevin you will always be number one in my eyes and the club, when it's run properly should offer you a life presidency or something like that! 'Toon Talk' still going strong and building up a good following thanks to nufc.com and Facebook! Regular contributors help the show flow and seems to be popular with a lot of ex-pats. Malaysia, USA, Australia. Geordies here Geordies there....

The International break does my head in. It's club before country for me every time. Even in those glory days when we had Beardsley Waddle and Gascoigne with three lions on their chest I'd rather hark back to happier times when they plied there trade at St James. Nowadays it's all initials. JT, FL, RF, what's that all about. No you can keep it for me. I'll tune into the World Cup like everyone else, probably for the same reason...there will be nowt else on. We now have two weeks without a game when what we really need is to take advantage of our good start. The two week break also means that apart from the usual rallying calls from JT and Co. we have to suffer fantasy island stories from the tabloids and various media outlets as they have nobody to speak to at the club. With the loan market opening for a month we are being linked with all and sundry. No that's not a Turkish international. Marlon Harewood, Marlon King, Marlon Brando. You name it, as long as he's called Marlon it seems. Xisco is making his mouth go from his new base. In a nutshell he says that he deliberately stopped playing at our club to engineer a move. Ha ha ha, did you notice? No me neither. More crap in the papers about Moat 'edging closer'. To what I ask? His front door? A mid-life crisis? The longer this drags on the less I believe it. I still fully expect Mike Ashley and Co. to be here for a long time to come.

Still no story of Mike Ashley streaking across the hallowed turf which is a relief. Cheryl Tweedy married to JT, FL, and RF's friend AC admits in a candid interview that she would buy the club if she had the wedge. Never write it off at this club. A consortium of Jimmy Nail, Brian Johnson, Sid The Sexist, Michelle Heaton, the Fat Slag's and Cheryl Tweedy. Imagine the boardroom Xmas party! More good news regarding Mike Ashley and Co. He is to be investigated by the office of fair trading regarding some alleged fixing of prices with replica shirts. It's an old story, as I'm sure I've heard rumours of this before. It's just the latest in a long line of things going wrong for Mike Ashley and Co. It would be great to laugh at all the bad news but if found guilty he could end up on B-Wing with Ronnie Barker and Co. and where exactly would that leave us? Anyone got the Fat Slag's number?

Still twiddling my thumbs with this bloody international break. I can now confirm that Shola will miss at the very least 8 weeks. So will Hughton go for a loan striker or stick with the lone Ranger, that's the big question. The muddy waters of what Mike Ashley and Co.'s defence will be at court are starting to clear with confirmation that he is fighting Keegan's claim of unfair dismissal with a claim of breach of contract. I'm expecting a dirty fight here to be honest. Still think that poison dwarf will start shit stirring over the next week or two. He's been unusually quiet our taxi driver bashing dwarf. More talk of an American takeover overtaking Barry Moat who is still edging closer! It's like potty training the bairn. If you want it buy it Barry man or come out and tell us that it's a crock of shit like we all suspect.

Our first trip to Europe since Dundee pre-season! Cardiff away at the Cardiff City Stadium. Another purpose built arena, but to be fair at least these lads fill it and we have an atmosphere to savour. A game where most of us expected old boy Michael Chopra to come back to haunt us but Talys and Collocini, yes I know unbelievable, sniffed him out early doors. Not only did Colo keep a clean sheet but he notched the only goal of the game to send our travelling army into a frenzy. The only sour point of the day was Captain Smith taking a second yellow for his first red of the season. It will only be a one game ban, but with a threadbare squad it will be interesting to see how we cope at Blackpool on Wednesday. Yes you read that right, Wednesday. What was a matter with a 3pm Saturday kick off like? We love a weekend down Blackpool. I'm sure this has been a conspiracy between the Police, Council and Fizzy Pop League. Talk now about Mike Ashley and Co. dropping the price of the club completely contradicting previous statements about £100 million or nothing. You just don't know what to believe. 'Don't believe the hype' I can hear blasting from a neighbours barbecue as I write this. Public Enemy, how apt. Also rumours of a new centre-half coming in on loan. Zurab Khizanishvili from Blackburn. He's a Georgian International, and not a very good one my boss Chris Kyle says who is a Rovers diehard.

It somehow felt strange to be heading down to the party capital of the North West knowing I wouldn't be falling down drunk in 'The Flagship' or 'The Tower Lounge' this time. Instead I fell down drunk at Bloomfield Road. In fact I'm pretty sure most of the team were drunk as we come away humbled with only Steve Harper and Jose Enrique coming away with any credit as we lost 2-1 with Andy Carroll grabbing our consolation. Candy floss anyone? Let's just hope Hughton can right the wrongs, kick a few up the backside and put the right team out against Plymouth on Saturday. Zurab arrives. If he is half as good as Temuri Ketsbaia I'll be well happy. I'm sure you lot will to. Never mind what my gaffer says eh?

Right on cue eh? Dennis Wise all over the papers and on Sky Sports News with quotes about his fall and fall at St James.

'The system imposed at Newcastle just did not work and it is as simple as that.'

'You are always going to get stick for everything you do.'

'People like to blame me for most things anyway.'

'It's important to keep some dignity and not shout off.'

To be fair to Wise, (and I don't like to be) these questions may have been sprung on him. He was covering a match on television. However the timing of his first appearance stinks to high heaven and looks like an attempt to undermine Keegan before the case starts. It's the first shot across the bows if you like. As I've already said I think these shots will go unanswered from Keegans' side as I'm sure what he has to say will prove his innocence and those keyboard warriors on

31

the message boards can ...well eat their keyboards.

Paul Whitehouse the funny part of the Enfield and Whitehouse show on BBC has been appearing in a series of adverts for an insurance company or something like that where he plays a few different characters. For a change it's not a Geordie that they have chosen to take the mick out of. Instead it's Plymouth fans, and the advert sees a Whitehouse playing a Plymouth fan picking up his mates for the away trip to Newcastle. The catchphrase the fan has is 'Green arrrrmy'. Needless to say every time toon fans bumped into their fans today they were greeted with a chorus of 'Green arrrmy!' I'm sure the novelty has already worn off for them. The game itself saw us put the Blackpool result behind us with another home win, 3-1 this time. Tayls getting the first after five minutes, and I expected the floodgates to open. They didn't and 'Green arrrmy' got level in the second half. We put the game to bed in the second half after the withdrawal of that footballing imposter Barton again, who just doesn't look interested. Nolan got us back in front with another goal my Gran Cecilia could have tucked away and Carroll wrapped up the points with a neat finish that bulged in the onion bag. (I love that.) Handy Andy could have had another but he hit the bar with an overhead kick that I would have scored in my prime ....on Fifa!

The papers lapping up the Mike Ashley and Co. v Keegan case. It's behind closed doors so how anyone knows what is going on is beyond me. Tales of Mike Ashley and Co. allegedly offering Keegan a pay-off outside court hit the front pages whilst troops die in Afghanistan and are cast aside to the inner pages. I guess those deaths just aren't important enough ey? Also rumours that the club could go into administration as Keegan wants £25 million pounds. This is a figure plucked from the sky surely? Ok I'll stop calling you Shirley! Seriously £25 million...where do they get that from. Sensational reporting as usual. I'm sure Kevin wants what is owed. £10 million seems too much, I'm expecting a £6 million pay-off, but as Peter Beardsley used to say in interviews, 'Time will tell.' Obviously. More talk that the takeover battle is heating up. Not at St James, but at 'bigger' clubs like Portsmouth, West Ham and Birmingham.

The tributes paid to Sir Bobby Robson over the last few weeks have been wonderful. He only had a short term at our club, but he was a 'Geordie' and a true fan not like the Blair's of this world. I have had a tear in my eye on more than one occasion when fans at other fixtures have had a minute's applause and sang his name. I suppose for us fans it's the equivalent of Diana dying for Royalists. It doesn't matter whether you knew him or met him...you just felt like you knew him or had met him. I met him a few times. Precious moments. The tribute at Durham Cathedral was mind blowing. I watched it on the box today and it was spot on. I noticed a few people in the crowd who blagged a ticket to the service. Fair play to them. I'd have loved to have been there. I was at St Nicholas in Newcastle in 1988 for Jackie Millburn's' funeral. Another monumental occasion. The tributes were deserved and even Gazza kept it together. RIP.

I told you...I told you...the bloody Carling Cup is jinxed for us. A 2-0 defeat at Peterborough with the bairns given a run out shows where our intentions lie. Promotion at the first attempt. Expect the same in the FA Cup in January. The worry is again though that if we get hit by a lot of injuries as we often do that the squad just can't handle it.

The is he isn't he scenario with Marlon Harewood is over as he has become our latest loan signing. He will go straight into the squad for our next fixture fittingly against Ipswich Town who have I'd say more of a hold over Sir Bobby than us. He won things here. He was Mr Ipswich.

Another Saturday teatime televised game. This one shown on that well known hotbed of football. BBC2. A friend's reunited moment for us with Roy Keane in the home dug-out. Oh how I wish Shearer could have been in our dug-out today. Looks like that particular stand off will have to wait for another decade. Pre-match and half-time tributes for Sir Bobby were well organised and well observed. Not even any abuse for Eric Gates. A resounding 4-0 away win for the lads and a hat-trick for Nolan. His first since he was 15 apparently? Why he chose to share that I'm not sure but well done all the same. Keano's face was a picture at the end. He must have gone through a box of chewing gum. Zurab had a steady game and Harewood featured but couldn't judge him today. Just enjoy it is my motto at the minute because knowing this lot there is a huge dip on our rollercoaster just around the corner. Ryan Taylor is now forgiven. He has now scored as many goals for us as he has scored against us as he grabs the third goal today.

Two home games now and a chance dare I say it to open a considerable gap on the chasing pack. First up Queens Park Rangers and then Bristol City. QPR will see the return of a good pal of mine Peter Ramage, but he's carrying a knock and says he's struggling. He's gutted to say the least.

I didn't catch up with 'Rammy' and he didn't play. Fair play to QPR they brought a large away following. They were arseholes but they brought a lot of arseholes. This maybe sour grapes from my point of view due to the fact that QPR actually played well tonight and deserved their point in the 1-1 draw. We played with no width or conviction and were poor. Nicky Butt on the left wing ? For fuck sake ? It appears that we went into this game over confident as a win would have put us 5 points clear at the top. In reality a point flattered us. Harewood grabbing a goal which yes my Gran could have poked home. Guthrie's penalty tickle was farcical. For someone who can really leather a ball he just struck this with no conviction. In fact my gran…ok…ok! As it's been said many a time this is a horrible league to get out of and I still think that there are more twists and turns to come. It's going to be a long hard season. Had to laugh at a new face behind me at the game. Sitting with his mate he commented on the game saying,

'This is wank'.

His mate said 'Proper.'

He then replied, 'Proper wank.'

He's done it again! Chris Hughton has been awarded Manager Of The Month again. I take my shoes off to him. (I don't wear hats). Sadly Shola was pipped for Player Of The Month this time, due to the fact that he was injured. I did wind my Rob up though by saying that the Fizzy Pop League had given it to him anyway. He didn't laugh.

Is this a our first blip of the season or the beginning of the end. 0-0 at home with Bristol City. Oh my god. Over 43,000 today can confirm that if we had been playing till midnight we would still fail to score. An entertaining game nonetheless but we need to win our home games and not lose away if we have any chance of bouncing back from the Fizzy Pop League at the first attempt.

Toon Talk hits 1500 listeners tonight. Good times!

Leam Lane
Just like Ally McCoist (when he was at Rangers)

Monday's annual Grange Villa Carnival had Newcastle triumph over Sunderland in the cricket competition. The Sunderland fans spent the day filling in domino cards in the bar by putting FTM instead of their names. You wouldn't really expect anything else to be honest.

Our last Tuesday night game of the season had us with a home fixture against Leam Lane. The opening minutes of the game had a little dog join in with us. The dog's owner wasn't too pleased. We then went a goal behind. Sharpey took a mega skepie and broke a bit of neighbour Bone Crusher Bob's fence by whacking a football at it. Dirty Den got scared.

30mins into the game we were shipping goals faster then it was raining and rain it did as we crumbled to a 1.3 half time score line. I hid inside a hedge, away from the rain and Sharpey.

The Ultras did however have the joy of welcoming former Villa player and local heartthrob Spike who turned up to watch the match. Spike used to get subbed with 20mins to go of each game he played so he could go to the Central Club to watch the strippers. He once missed an important cup game as he was building a shed.

He now has strippers performing in his shed on a weekly basis.

Skipper Brown pushed an opponent from the pitch and shouted at the lad 'your as week as piss, this is a man's game' this action lead to a Villa revival and a bit of fight back. Another DC penalty (DC likes taking penalty's as he can't be caught off-side) and a double strike from Chrisy P put us into a 4.3 lead. Chrisy P's 1st was a thunderbolt strike in the style of Ally McCoist (when he was at Rangers). Maybe Singe and Clak had to eat a slice of humble pie for laughing last week.

The game apparently finished as a 4.4 draw I don't know this as it got dark and I couldn't see.

After the game it was a rush for Singe and Podge to get through to Wrekington as the Villa were up in front of the management committee for the heinous crime of playing an ineligible player. That player was Chris Clues who's actually been playing football at the Villa for 4 seasons. I know Sharpey in his Bobby Robson mode often call's Chris, Steven which we still find funny but this I'm afraid this wasn't the problem. Top and bottom of the story is that Singe failed to sign on Cluey as he was too busy writing shit and taking photographs. Cluey failed to sign a form as he was eating wine and drinking cheese (or something like that). The end result for the Villa is a thirteen million pound fine (£30) and a deduction of 3 valuable points. Is the season fucked already? To add further insult to injury according to the dithery old men of the league's officials I'm not very good as Grange Villa Secretary

Bad times.

Saltwell
Condom

In all fairness it's been a difficult week for me and Grange Villa Football Club. Maybe on a par with the time I gave the ball away in the last minute and Sunniside equalised. Or the time I scored an own goal when I played for The Board Inn. It didn't help that the goalkeeper that day was one of Newcastle's hardest pub doormen.... And he wasn't very happy with me (first and last time I played in the back four).

Anyway this week has seen me chuck a bit of a hissy fit

37

in good old Kevin Keegan style; I'd like to say thanks to those who have given kind words of encouragement.

Is having a fucking hobby supposed to be such hard work?

Today had us off to deepest darkest Gateshead to play football in a salt mine against Saltwell Club. Has the drink culture problem at this football team been eradicated? Main culprits Skipper Brown spent his night visiting a museum then watch X-Factor, Singe went to a leek show with his wife!

Sharpey has a new washing machine so Clak doesn't have to wash the strips any more. Singe put his old washer on the drive for the gypsies to take away. Apparently Pelton is full of them; it's also full of women in their pyjamas going shopping as well.

The Villa Ultras returned from there jaunt to Magaluf at 7am fair play to Stupid Ben for turning up for the match. He did however have a big complaint about the culinary delights of Spanish cooking. It's been over 2 weeks since he last had a proper Sunday Dinner. He had to pay 10euros for the world's worst dinner where he alleged that the Yorkshire Pudding on his plate had already had a bite out of it and the gravy had curdled. Not sure how gravy curdles mind.

To prove this fact he showed off his holiday snaps on his phone which were all of this dinner. Hopefully his Ma makes up for this 2 week food drought today. Stupid Ben also announced that he bought a laser pen from a lucky-lucky man; it can shine a beam that can be seen up to 5 miles away. It also carry's enough radiation to burst balloons.

But not footballs!

DC after undertaking a meaty challenge was called a 'fat

twat' by a Saltwell defender. They obviously don't know that DC goes to weight watchers during the week and has managed to lose 3 pounds. The Villa bandit is most grateful for this.

The result was an entertaining 0.0 draw zzzzzz. An unusual score line for this level of football. Slug, new lad Chris Guy and Fireman Scott were all in good form at the back.

The trip home had Slug Marshall throw several Lucozade filled condoms at DC's car along The Team Valley. DC didn't get mad....much.

Leam Lane – 1st Division cup 1st Round (match off)
Game off

Every Sunday morning before football I like a little pick me up.

A legal one I have to add.

I've stopped at the local shop every Sunday morning for the last 2 years for a bottle of a famous brand of 'energy sports drink'.

I do this not in the hope I get a game of football or that it makes me play better I do this as far as I can tell is a good hangover cure.

For 2 years I've tried so hard to engage the shop keeper in polite small talk.

I can't even muster a simple good morning, thank you or goodbye from the above mentioned shop keeper.

I pay 99p for this 'energy sports drink'.

Over the 2 years I've spent approximately £47.52.

I was in a large global supermarket chain store at the weekend and found a 6 pack of the above mentioned 'energy sports drink' for £2.00.

I'm sorry if I've gone off on a tangent on this one but money isn't the issue here, manners and being civil to a customer are.

Both cost nothing.

Well in reality they have cost something, a hefty £47.52 as I won't be shopping in my local again.

Giant capitalistic consumer groups win again?

Anyway rant over, back to today's events

Today's cup game against Leam Lane was called off at the last minute after we had travelled all the way to Heworth. The pitch was double booked with a team from The Tyneside League.

A flip of a coin had our game lose and the Tyneside game given the go ahead.

We then tried to get into Leam Lane Club for a 10.30am pint but we were told to come back at 12pm. This left 17 very unhappy men bumbling around the streets of Gateshead. Somebody then came up with a fantastic idea of actually going home. This was in all fairness a bloody good idea and exactly what we did.

Leam Lane – 1st Division cup 1st Round
Run

Last week's postponed cup game against Leam Lane was hastily re-arranged for today with our derby match against Lumley getting re-arranged for later in the season.

This in theory was okay, however The Great North Run caused us a logistical problem with all the direct roads to the pitch being closed. A hefty detour of the outlying regions of Wardley and Heburn was needed including some serious of road driving. Luckily they were no Red Indians on the road that early just 54,000 fucking stupid joggers.

I fail to see the point of running from Newcastle to South Shields in a pair of shorts and a vest.

In my illustrious footballing career I ran around the opposition's 18yard box very infrequently. Running is not fun.

A depleted Villa side this week due to Sir Barrington and Marc Ward looking at babies, Speed Y Jelly having a cricked neck (who was in Tenerife having treatment). Fireman Scott was rescuing cats from trees and putting out fires Chris Guy was drunk and Tinhead was sucking on lumps of Edam in Amsterdam or whatever it is he does for a living. The most bizarre absence of the day was Young Pyle who Sharpey instead of using him in the squad for today's game had him laying wooden flooring in his own house. Perks of being the boss?

Thankfully Stupid Ben was back from injury as was Hardy. Stupid Ben has spent the week cutting down trees with an axe at The Villa woods just to get back to match fitness.

The bloke who opens up the changing rooms for Leam Lane failed to show up some say he was still in bed. I hope he got lucky as this unfortunately had 22 blokes stripping off in the street.

Not ideal.

Certainly not ideal when Lee McGuiness's girlfriend had to look at Hardy's willy which was on show more than usual. The goat that was tethered up behind the changing rooms last time we played here had amazingly turned into a chicken. The chicken then got chased around by Hardy (who else). The chicken thankfully managed to escape. It's all good clean animal fun around here.

Slug Marshall had a wee on the pitch as Sharpey gave his pre-match team talk and DC announced to us that he's lost another 3 pounds this week. He's now the 3rd fattest player at the Villa. The famous Saturday night Grange Villa drink culture gang were full of tall tales of drinking Brown Ale before yesterdays Newcastle match with former Everton striker Kevin Campbell as well as The Geordie Dancer. However Kevin Campbell's striper girlfriend's titty's were much better to look at than the Geordie Dancer's.

The game itself we found ourselves 2.0 up after the first 5mins of the game playing breathtaking beautiful football. This however was as good as it got. The next 115mins of football from us was nothing other than rancid dog shit. All 14 players used today should hang their heads in shame as we crashed to an unacceptable 3.2 extra time defeat. The cup I can safely say will not be going to The Villa this year.

All the best to Leam Lane for the rest of the competition.

Hardy making his come back from his dislocated shoulder was subbed due to having a blister on his foot. His replacement was a lad called Boris who is studying hairdressing at University he also announced that he hasn't played football since he was 16 and didn't know which position he plays in. A useful lad to have in the squad then. Singe then bust Hardy's blister with a tin opener. The biggest complaint of the day was from Stupid Ben who was deeply unhappy about the game going to extra time. He hates nothing more on earth than a Sunday dinner re-heated in the microwave. As we all know this action curdles the gravy.

I left Sharpey and Old Pyle in Leam Lane Club (it was

open this week) watching a Country and Western band. By this time I'd had more than I could take of today. Next year I'm going to do the Great North Run instead.

Saltwell – Bob Curry Cup 1st Round

Saltwell – Bob Curry Cup 1st Round
Dead Rabbit Sandwiches'

The end of September and The Villa are struggling 3rd bottom of the league and out of the realistically only winnable cup competition of the season 'The race for the Premiership' now looks like a mythical dream. Today we yet again entertained them Salty Seadog's of Saltwell Social Club in the all league affair of the Bob Curry Cup. Barry from the Thomas Wilson commented to me during the week that we should merge sides and have one fuck of enormous squad and then still be shit.

Things are not going well at camp Villa.

Stupid Ben's weekly keep fit routine of chopping down trees in the Villa has unfortunately come to an end as his Mam has took his axe off him, he also announced that his ankle was giving him a bit of stick from an injury picked up ice skating last night. He's such a cultured boy.

It turns out that we at the Villa not only have to put up with an epidemic amount of dog shit on the pitch we now have the added bonus of having dead rabbits as well (it was also unproven that local hunter Chris Smith shot the animal). The ever exocentric Sharpey told us that he likes nothing better than a dead rabbit sandwich. I'm however not sure an alive rabbit sandwich would be the same for Sharpey or the rabbit.

Goat Mitchell was back in the bosom of the Villa Ultras today having being missing for a few weeks. Apparently last week he was in Gateshead throwing berries at some runners in the Great North Run.

Scratchy Howey showed off his new tattoo on his back it looked like it had been done with a hot spoon and a Bic Biro.

A much much improved Villa performance from the last few weeks had us saunter to a welcome 5.2 victory. Could the cup be coming to Chester Le Street this year?

I'm afraid Podge but if we actually win the Bob Curry Cup we are presented with a cup and not a plate of Beef Madras and Egg Pilau Rice.

Bob Curry to the best of my knowledge is not a relation to the angry, ball greedy, hyper active, ginger, ice hockey loving, flabby bellied Darren Curry from Grange Villa who goes by the name of DC. He was missing today due to some problem with his freezer and a carton of Ben and Jerry's melting on the kitchen floor (is this the start of the excuses for not coming to football?)

During the game Hardy wiped snots on Sharpey jumper.
Sharpey then smacked Hardy's bottom.
Hardy followed this up by kicking a football at Sharpey.
They both shook hands and said sorry.
End of the stupidity?
No
Back at the club Hardy put a chicken drumstick in Sharpy's pint.
Sharpey said 'I will get the fucker back'
At this point I went home; I have better things to do on a Sunday afternoon.

OCTOBER

A full time manager!

Another International break for JT and CO. to revel in their own glory. We won't win it you do know that don't you?

I foolishly booked my holidays a week after international week, after a mix up at Wraith HQ! So had to miss not just one but three games in total. At least our constant coverage on television worked in my favour this time with the Nottingham Forest game being beamed out to millions across the world...oh and me in Parma Mallorca. I say me because in Club Martha's television lounge there was just me watching. That was until about ten minutes into the game when a French guy and his female friend walked in, looked me up and down and then looked at the screen in disgust. I had my toon top on. Had shaved my nappa and my flies were up. I'd even used the bairns baby wipes on my addidas trainers to clean off last night's slops. Anyway off he went to the bar, and in a broken English asked if he could change the channel over. The Spanish waiter said that the guy who changed the television over wasn't in yet. Wonder how you describe his job at the job centre? 'Chief Televisual Operator'? Anyway I digress. This put my back up to be honest. As it would. The French connection chose to sit just behind me with aforementioned female. The game to be fair was enough to turn a man to drink, so I ordered another San Miguel as Francois bore a hole in the back of my head. We were really under the cosh without Tayls and Colo, and they may be out for a few weeks so we are really going to get tested now. As half-time approaches Dawn and Rebecca my Mrs and the Bairn turn up to go for our scran. I order them a swift one to get me through to the interval. Dexter Blackstock beats the offside trap and nudges the ball past Harper to give them the lead. I'm gutted. Heads in my hands whilst my daughter just under three shouts 'Goal!' She will learn bless her. The Frenchman has a wry smile, which is soon wiped off his face as his Parisian beauty orders him to buy her something to eat in the adjoining room as she is bored and he hasn't even bought her a drink. I then in turn have a wry smile as he passes our table. The ref blows his whistle and with that I'm off like Linford Christie with Dawn and Becks in tow to the Buffett. I cram two buns down my throat with a bit of steak and butter in between and then like a News Of The World reporter in a brothel make my excuses and leave to get back to the television room for the second half. My wry smile broadens with crumbs dropping from the crevices in my face as I see my French counterpart tucking into his main course, still the stitch I had was worth it. As I got back to my seat I was horrified to see that the channel had been switched over and for what? Egg chasing! Bloody rugby. Toulouse against Lyon. I hot footed it straight to the bar and asked the 'Chief Televisual Operator' to put the match back on. He remembered me and said 'Ok no problem'. I got back to my seat in time to see Captain Smith kick off the second half. I ordered another San Miguel and savoured the sweet taste of victory against the French again. You might as well get a desert and coffee mate. We rallied in the second half and were all over the 'Tricky Trees' like a rash. We just couldn't finish our dinner, unlike our French friend who was cursing his luck and my skills at eating two buns in the buffet in a world record time. The Frenchman did have the last laugh I'm sad to say when I had one of those embarrassing moments that you can only have when watching the match on television in a bar where you are the only person supporting a team. Nolan scores to level. I shout, jump, and wail and whoop like a banshee and wolf combined...only to see the bloody flag raised and the 'goal' wiped out. I just wanted the ground to open up and swallow me and my pint up. Forest held out and I suppose Nolan's pre-match quote that 'If Forest beat us their fans will celebrate as if they have won the European Cup', may have stoked up the fires before the game. After the match goalscorer Blackstock admitted that he thought the comments were 'disrespectful'. He also questioned how many times Newcastle had won the European Cup? No answer to that really. We deserved at least a point though, and didn't get it. Two points out of nine. No manager of the month this time for Hughton, but whispers in the Spanish version of 'The Daily Star' that he may be about to land the manager's job fulltime. So my prophecy of Mike Ashley and Co. staying on maybe about to come true! Someone please wake me up from this nightmare.

Texts home can't confirm or deny the Hughton whisper. I have a sleepless night tossing and turning. Next day the Spanish version of 'The Daily Star' carries the headline 'Toon Job All Yours Hughton'. Ian Murtagh is never often wrong and he confirms that Hughton has been summoned for a meeting with the board. He is quoted as saying 'The discussions relate to turning my temporary role into a permanent one.' As I read the story Chris the Scouse lad in the next room peeps over the balcony to say that there are quotes in the Spanish version of 'The News Of The World' attributed to Mike Ashley without the Co. He confirms that Barry Moat has been bugging him for two years. He is laying it on the line to him. He wants £80 million up front from him and is willing to wait for the rest. He also says that if this demand can't be met then he is considering staying on. So not edging closer then Barry? This is just further confirmation to me that this whole scenario has been a sham from start to finish. I'm gutted. This once great club of ours has darker days to come I fear. I like Chris Hughton. He has done the best with what he has got, but the final quote attributed to Mike Ashley without the Co. is quite chilling. He will have the final say on players.

The FA Arbitration Panel rule in favour of Kevin Keegan. Surprise, surprise. Where's Cilla Black when you need her? Special K is completely vindicated whilst our club and its owners are called liars by the panel. Keegan's statement is short and to the point.

"I resigned because I was being asked to sanction the signing of a player in order to 'do a favour' for two South American agents. No one at the club had seen this player play and I was asked to sign him on the basis of some clips on You Tube. This is something that I was not prepared to be associated with in any way. The club knew that I objected strongly to this transfer and were aware that by continuing with it I was likely to feel that I had no option but to resign. Notwithstanding this, they went onto sign the player at a very substantial cost to the club. The allegation made in the press that I turned down an offer of £4m to settle the claim is simply untrue. No such offer was made to me. I would like to thank the fans of Newcastle United for their continued support and wish them and the club continued success in the current season in their goal of reaching the Premier League."

Leaves a lump in my throat that. I'm not going to dwell on this but the club admitted that they fed the media stories which were untrue, calling them an exercise in public relations. How can we believe anything that Mike Ashley and Co. say ever again? What do you mean you didn't anyway?

Gareth ran the 'Toon Talk' show without me and after initial problems he cruised through it and it went well. Well done mate. I'll be back next week mate.

Will the real Newcastle United please stand up? Total crisis and I'm stuck in a foreign land paying over the top for papers and the internet! Another defeat this time at the hands of the mighty 'Scunthorpe'. The lads I've met in the hotel all try to sympathise with me but as one is a Leeds fan and the other a Hull fan I can just tell that they are dying to laugh out loud. I console myself with a 'molly' cocktail whilst dancing with my 2 year old daughter at the hotel disco. My wife then informs me that my cocktail is non alcoholic. They say it comes in threes! As the disco starts to heat up, (well as much as a kids disco can) we suffer a Scottish invasion of 'Braveheart' proportions. Kids in football kits too old for the disco start to move onto the dance floor. Tables and chairs are moved and upturned and there are no parents to be seen. One lad attempts to squeeze through the smallest gap in the world between our table almost causing drinks to fly. I ask him to watch what he's doing and low and behold the mother appears. Needless to say the third 'event' had arrived, and after a verbal exchange which did nothing for Anglo/Scottish relations I gathered my family together and head off to the room. I blame Chris Hughton for this. Stories coming via text and email from a couple of the lads down at Scunny say Mike Ashley had a run in with a few fans outside the ground. With something like this I'd expect at least a bit of mobile phone footage, but nothing. Another bit of spin methinks? Nolan proving to be a key player this season with another goal, albeit a consolation.

The final game of my holiday ends in a win! Yes a win against Doncaster! Has the tide turned back in our favour? My dad and Rob are honest in their respective reports. 'We were crap.' Match reports suggest they are correct. 'Newcastle humping the ball aimlessly up field to the forwards.' Goals from Carroll and Nolan seal the points though and stops the rot, Kishnavili gets a red card. A penalty miss from Doncaster helps us out as well. It balances out over the course of a season Donny fans honest. That's what people told me last season and I'm still waiting! Now last minute checks, passport, tickets, case, daughter, wife....I'm comin' home Newcastle!

I have arrived home to another Mike Ashley And Co. classic. As expected Hughton is confirmed now as manager. No problem with that under the circumstances. Mike Ashley has withdrawn the club from the market. No problem with that as I didn't think it was up for sale in the first place. Newcastle United to sell the naming rights of the ground to the highest bidder. No pro....WHAT!!!!?? My mobile goes mad as does my better half, (your not even off the plane yet and it's started /repeat to fade) and I nearly collapse in the airport with the pressure of being a Newcastle United fan. The texts fly in from Sunderland fans that I know with side splitting suggestions. I crave a bucket of molly cocktail to take me away from this madness. I get home unpack the case and then start to read the countless chronicles my mother in law has saved for me to catch up on recent events that the Spanish papers would deem unimportant.

Newcastle United Supporters Trust really starting to get their show on the road. They have launched a petition against the re-naming of the ground. 15,000 signatures already! Great way to get a database to lads! Murmurings of a campaign to buy the club to. Be great if it could work. I have more faith in this then Graham Roberts gang. What happened to them anyway? Watch this space.

Everyone having there say about the name change. Ant, Dec oh and Freddie Shepherd. Good old Fred. He says it's a disgrace. I really do wish he would just keep his nose out. I know how it works. A story breaks, He gets a call. He does the interview and it's edited by the news channel without his final approval. After everything that's gone on with him and the club though you think he would just keep his nose out wouldn't you.

The Stella
Two nil down, four three up, Grange Villa are on the up
Stupid Ben has a new job.

He now dig's holes in roads with West Yorkshires chief hole digger our very own Sharpey.

Sharpey actually made me some breakfast this morning. He made me a cheese muffin but forgot to put any cheese on it. Never mind.

Apparently Stupid Ben came to work on his first day with no safety boots. When asked where his boots were he replied 'I have some boots but there in the back yard at home. I can't wear them as their full of spider's webs and leaves from trees. I will however be able to wear them tomorrow as I will have my best socks on'. Not sure how the spiders feel in having to find a new home and exactly what 'best sock's' are

Back to today's events we made our first trip to The Northumbria Centre (The Hackney Marshes of the North East) of the season where we played the Stella freshly relegated from The Premier League last season.

That's Stella as in Stella Maris Catholic Club from Washington and not Stella Artois the famous lager first brewed in Louvain, Belgium in 1926 as a Christmas brew. The word Stella is of course Latin for star.

The star of this game today was not Chrisy P (the best looking lad at the Villa) who claimed he was off to Barcelona for what he calls a mid season international break. However his girlfriend Jessica said they were going to Salou. In reality we don't have a clue to his exact location other than he wasn't at football. Fireman Scott was again missing as he was putting out...em....fires. DC was still having ice cream related issues. Is this season going to be the same as his other season's where he plays the first half dozen games then can't be arsed to turn up again?

Another mix up with double booked changing rooms and our still 'slightly damp' strips didn't do well for out pre-match preparation as we tumbled to going 2 goals down.

Chris Guy 'did' his ankle in after 9mins and now has a lump the size of a small South American country. He was replaced by the ancient Podge who put in a retro 90's style, man of the match performance and capped his game of with a 900 yard wonder goal which turned the game around to a thumping 4.3 victory for the Villa. Are things on the up for The Villa?

Baby Geoffrey made his debut for The Villa Ultras on the side lines at the youthful age of 1 he has more hair than his dad Speed Y Jelly and probably talks more than him as well.

In all fairness Speed Y Jelly was also awesome today he should have been a Roman gladiator. When his missus Catherine was asked if Speed Y Jelly was as good in bed as he was on a football pitch her reply was a simple 'no'.

Scruffy Spice Haley also hurt his ankle and hopped around the centre circle for 5 minutes as if his polio shoe had come off.

The leader of The Villa Ultras Goat Mitchell who once punched Ex Villa player Swamp Donkey for being crap spent the full 90mins of today's match playing games on Scratchy Howey's iphone. He thinks football is now boring and not violent enough for his likening.

Washington Highwayman
Spit, punch, defeat

Tuesday night's league meeting had Singe yet again in trouble with the officials of the league he was almost horse whipped and left hanging from a lamppost outside The Stormont Main Club for a misinterpretation of a recent letter. League Secretary Happy Harry wasn't overly happy. It's canny safe to say that the secretary of the year yet again won't be coming to Grange Villa this season.

Who are all these men you see early on a Sunday morning hanging around empty pub car parks, they're all bleary eyed and always to be found clutching sports bags. They then all get into cars and head off into the distance in convoy.

They're part of a dying breed in the Xbox culture of the fat, lazy youth of today.

They're what's known as Sunday League Footballers.

In 2008/09 England had 31,942 Sunday morning football teams, this has greatly declined over the last 10 years or so. It shows the strength and attraction of the Gateshead League where 3 new teams have joined up for this season. One of these new teams is another bunch of highwaymen to go with them lot from Whickham, this time it was our turn to take on the Washington version. Washington Highwayman are doing well this season sitting in the lofty heights of 3rd place, a place we can only dream to be at the moment. We would have to raise our game today and have the side at its full strength and not to have lads out on the piss. There is also no truth whatsoever that Skipper Brown, Hardy, Boy Whitfield plus Hood and Hend from The Ultras were out 'doing' a 14-hour bender yesterday in 70's style clothes for Singe's birthday. Mr Sharpe if you're reading this we were all tucked up in bed by 11pm

Obviously not in the same bed as that would be....well....emm...fruity.

Goat Mitchell has packed in being leader of the Ultras and now wants to spend his Sunday's riding around the pitch on a motorbike. He wants to be known as Thunder Mitchell from now on. Boy Whitfield had to play in goal again and was helpless to prevent us crashing to a 5.3 defeat. He did however nearly shoot a pigeon out of the sky with a goal kick.

There is talk flying around that The Villa are going to get a stand built at the pitch, it would of course have to be named after long standing manger Neill Sharpe and go by the name of The Sharpe End.

Slug Marshall now runs like a fatter version of Robocop (but not as fat as Kebabcop) although he did get punched in the face by an opponent. Former Stanley League Referee George the Bear came to watch today's game and did nothing other than gay wrestle Scruffy Haley and fart. He then threatened to arrest the kid who punched Marshall. Remember that George is a prison warden and has no legal powers of arrest.

Sharpey has also reverted back to his nasty habit of spiting on the ground when he gets angry. He did a lot of spitting today

Peartree
All the sevens

The Peartree has a nice sound to it, you think of hot, lazy, summer days in an orchard. Or even a bottle of this new fangled cider everybody's drinking. You know the stuff where you put half a ton of ice in a pint glass before gulping it down.

In reality The Peartree are of course Heworth Ship who have changed their name for this season. There are obviously no pear trees in the Villa or any trees of any description as Stupid Ben has unfortunately from an arboricultural point of view got his axe back at this rate Oliver's Tree Services will be out of business.

Sharpey came to football with a fuzzy beard looking like an ice road trucker along with the return of DC. He admitted that he'd been missing the past few weeks due to Tesco's 2 for 1 offer on Ben and Jerry's ice cream. Newcastle striker Marlon Harwood came to watch today's game, but then we realised it was actually a plank of wood from neighbour Bone Crusher Bob's broken fence.

Hood strangely announced to us that he wants Sir Alan Sugar for a Dad for no other reason other than the fact that he looks like a nice bloke. I don't think Hood understands the implication of having a sugar daddy.

Thunder Mitchell was again undertaking his football exile he went all the way to Catterick Market for a pork sandwich. He commented the other week that football wasn't violent enough for him anymore; well he missed a bramer of a fight today.

Sir Barrington's No 4 shirt needed emergency treatment as it was torn in half as a 22 man brawl popped up from nowhere just before half time. The Peartree obviously took the hump with The Villa cruising to an easy 3.0 half time score line and DC in inspirational form (for once); this resulted in a defender punching our ice cream loving Canadian in the head. All hell broke lose and it was a scene straight out of a Benny Hill sketch. After things had calmed down the referee rightly sent off Mr Punch and the game restarted with a free kick to The Peartree, who promptly went up the other end of the pitch and scored via Skipper Brown receiving another sly whack to the side of the head.

Half time and the ineffective Hardy was replaced by Scratchy Howey. Hardy if you want to sit up until 5am drinking vodka then you're going to be shit at football the next morning. Maybe him being sick before the start of the game when he should have been putting up the nets was an indication to how he was going to play today.

The second half again had the Villa in fine form as more goals rattled in as we ran out easy 7.1 winners. To keep in line with the number 7, Stupid Ben's number 7 shirt was the next to get ripped to bits; they are a nice bunch of lads. Boy Whitfield's grandma is going to have a lot of sewing work to do this week.

Winlaton West End
Dogs
Off to the mountainous region of High Spen today to play another new team to the league in the shape of Winlaton West End.

Noticeable absentees today were Sharpey; he was missing due to an emergency hole digging session in Huddersfield. I'm glad he wasn't there today actually as I'm sure he would have insisted on singing 'East End Boys and West End Girls' all the way up to the game. Sharpey as we know has always had a soft spot for 80's puffter music. Cluesy it was believed was at a wine and cheese party in Blackpool and big DC was doing his usual play one miss 6 trick.

High Spen of course is a million miles away from the Villa and a trillion miles above sea level. Thankfully it's too early for snow however when you play footballs on the side of mountains the pitch is never straight. The game only went ahead today due to some hard work behind the scenes from Happy Harry the league secretary in finding us a referee at the last moment due to Mr Strother our designated ref being away on holiday. In an end to end game we eventually came unstuck with a 5.3 defeat which in all fairness could have gone either way. Winlaton are a canny side and have adapted to the league well.

Never mind.

Some trivia from today Chrisy P made his 100th appearance for The Villa. Has there ever been a better looking lad to don the famous green strip? A little dog in a Newcastle United doggy jacket that was at the game certainly thought so. Good job Slug Marshall was still getting changed when the dog turned up as he has a past history of 'dognapping'.

It's also official Baby Geoffrey has more hair than Speed Y Jelly. Speedy Y Jelly also said his first words ever on a football pitch in the 8 years he's played for us. It sounded like 'fuck' but could actually have been 'muck'. Nobody is quite sure.

Substitute Scruffy Hailey got covered in sticky jacks from looking in the bushes for stray footballs and Fireman Scott's Dad's Bovril is so good you can actually run cars from off it.

No Thunder Mitchell I hear you ask, yes he was yet again missing from the side lines due to some overindulgence at Blue Bamboo's foam party last night. Not sure if he took his motorbike with him.

NOVEMBER

Its St James Park

A nice way for Chris Hughton to open his account a 1-0 win at Sheffield United. South Yorkshire police are as welcoming as ever and as helpful as ever. A fortuitous goal by Ryan Taylor with a wicked deflection seals the points. Don't forget though Sheffield United fans these things balance out over the course of the season. Did I tell you I'm still waiting for the balance to be addressed from last season? Andy Carroll came of age tonight in his battle with Sheffield 'hard man' Morgan. He gave as good as he got and led the line superbly. I think we have our next number 9 here. Loving the 'Supermac' sideburns by the way. Watching the replays Morgan may be credited with an own goal tonight.

The FA Cup draw gives us Plymouth Argyle away. Happy New Year.

Mike Ashley and Co. Push Derek Llambias out of their hidey hole to try and justify the re-naming of our ground. In a 'Chronicle Exclusive' Dekka says...

"What we are offering is a package. At the moment we have Sportsdirect.com signs all around the stadium which is what we will be offering to the sponsors should they wish to purchase that package.

"We are not getting rid of the St James' Park name; we are offering people the chance to have their branding all around the stadium as well as on a new jumbo electronic scoreboard. The company can then say it is whatever at St James' Park.

"To use an analogy, if you look at Gordon Ramsey's restaurant at Claridges, nobody calls it that, they don't call it Ramsey's at Claridges, they just call it Claridges and that will be the same with St James' Park."

Yippeeeee!!!! A jumbo scoreboard...well that's alright then! Hope it's like the 83-84 promotion season with those little blokes on jumping up and down when we score, and the Kenny Everet clapping hands. Oh and don't forget the pictures of those who had scored and we all had to guess who on earth it was!

Dekka continued in his 'Chronicle Exclusive'.

"All of the money that is raised will go straight back into the team and help us move forward as a business. We have taken a big hit this year following relegation and that hit has had to be covered by Mike because we have not got the full amount of money from the bank.

"We have to look at ways to increase our income and these sponsorship packages are a good way to do that. But we know the St James' Park name is part of the history of the club, part of its tradition, and we do not want to lose that."

As 100 flying pigs circle St James Park Dekka concludes that the money will go straight back into the team. Let's see what January brings. Hold on I can hear a band playing 'believe it if you like'... always liked that song.

Peterborough United at home today and a perfect example of how to vent your spleen at your owners and support your team at the same time. I took in the NUST flag today and got it along the Gallowgate End in a fashion. Smuggling it in was a job in itself. The Flag is huge and it burst my coat. So a quick coat swap with my dad and a bit of distracting of the stewards at our turnstile by Dad and Rob helped me in. My sudden weight gain looked far from convincing. Still we got it in and managed to fly the flag for the trust before a couple of overzealous stewards confiscated it. The team cruised to a 3-1 win without even getting out of 1st gear, and Gutierrez broke his league duck with a goal to savour. No sign of the famous Spiderman mask though which was the biggest disappointment of the day. It has most likely dissolved after so much time in his keks. Carroll again with a goal and Danny Simpson scores a goal that only full-backs seem to score. Must have been a cross! Not another game for over 2 weeks for us now as England force us to suffer another pointless friendly. This time Brazil. I can't wait.

The Newcastle United Supporters Trust (NUST) have launched the 'Yes We Can Campaign' to attempt to take ownership of the club. It's a big ask, but one I'm willing to support. Let's face it, what's the alternative? There are some good people involved in the movement, and some who I maybe haven't seen eye to eye with over the years, but for a change, we are all playing for the same side. Our team seems to be 'united' on the pitch, and at last us, the supporters, are getting 'united' off it. Mark Jensen who is at the forefront of the campaign had this to say.

"Its clear that we have no knight in shining armour to end the charade at St James' Park so we must look at how we can do this ourselves.

"The club is a fantastic investment if run properly and we aim to attract the type of investors who will seek to bring back the values of integrity and honesty to the club.

"We've been in discussions with serious people in the city and beyond and they have thrown down the gauntlet to supporters to lead the charge."

Chris Hughton chips in with his half penneth in the Journal on the stadium naming issue.

"I am quite sure that in a year's time, two years' time, 10 years' time, people will still refer to the stadium as St James'," he said. "It's not like a club that has actually moved its stadium. I can understand where the supporters are coming from, but in everybody's eyes, it will still be St James."

Everyone else has an opinion to it seems, and once again Mike Ashley and Co. Manage to get our proud club front page instead of back page. Chelsea make some noises about doing the same at Stamford Bridge and some cricket ground says they are up for destroying decades of history to. Mike Ashley and Co will no doubt be delighted that others are jumping on the band wagon of this fool hardy scheme.

Still no football. These bloody international breaks really do my head in. I pity Lee Ryder at the Chronicle, having to fill three pages on Newcastle United when there's nothing going on. Shola apparently targeting the Swansea game for his comeback at the end of the month, let's just hope he hits the ground running again. More transfer rumours beginning to circulate. Old boy Gary Caldwell, now at Celtic, is being linked with an emotional return to his former club. A step backwards surely. Meanwhile French winger Fabrice Pancrate who has been on trial at the club has impressed Alan Thompson in a run out for the second string. A player coming in? Surely not!

A full weekend of fixtures. 3pm Saturday kick offs...pies and Bovril...but not for us. Another bloody two days to wait for our trip to Preston which is to be televised live on Sky. I bet the big wigs are really disappointed that we are top of the table. They will have been praying for us to do a Leeds live to the universe as everyone predicted. Unlucky! Our reserve goalkeeper Fraser Forster has been having the time of his life on loan at Norwich. Seven clean sheets in twelve games for the youngster. He has agreed to stay at Carrow Road (it is still called that isn't it?) till the end of the season. Pancrate completes his move to us from PSG. He has signed until the end of the season.

Shola Ameobi has declared an interest in playing for Nigeria causing uproar as it would mean he would miss almost all of our fixtures in January because of the African Nations Cup! He is quoted in the Chronicle saying, "2010 is a big year for Nigeria. The African Nations Cup is the same for us as the European Championships is in Europe. It's a tournament I would love to play in. Bloody great news.

Boring boring Newcastle! But who cares. Another 1-0 win on the road at perennial play-off botherers Preston sees us regain top spot with Kevin Nolan grabbing a stupendous winner after good work by Harewood. Its Nolan's ninth of the season and one of his most important to date. It was a feisty game with plenty of incident and once again Alan Smith showed that he is a natural born leader at this level. Preston attempted to get Smith sent off for leading with his arm whilst he was competing for a header but the referee wasn't having any of it. Well done that man.

The loan window closed today without us bothering to sneak anybody in. It re-opens in February apparently. It's the first I had heard of it today. With all these bloody windows opening and closing no wonder its bloody cold. A contingent of former Newcastle Legends including Alan Shearer and Gazza hand in our forms for our World Cup bid at Wembley. Let's hope it's a success and the Makem bid falls flat on its face. All they have done is copy our blueprint. Mike Ashley and Co. visited the United training ground today, flying in by helicopter, allegedly to discuss transfer targets with manager Chris Hughton. Apparently they didn't stay long. Says it all really. Going to be a quiet January! More talk in the Chronicle today about Matt Kilgallon being a nailed on certainty in the transfer window. I'll believe it when I see it.

Swansea at home today and another easy home win. Pre-Match Jonas Gutierrez had pledged to bring out his mask again if he got his name on the score sheet. Good news...praying actually works...Harewood with two goals and Loverkrands the other despatch the Welsh sheep botherers 3-0. Mike Ashley and Co. Release a bit of propaganda via the official programme in Dekkas column.

"As you know, Mike made it clear after the end of last season that he was trying to sell the club and although there were a number of interested parties, none of them were able to match the £100m asking price. As a result, Mike decided that the best course of action, one that would put the welfare of the club at the top of the agenda, would be to remove the club from the market and concentrate solely on the aim that everyone connected with the club passionately desires - promotion straight back to the Premier League. His commitment is unwavering and the additional large sums of money he has recently pumped into the club amply demonstrate that."

It's becoming a war of words with the NUST sure to fire

a verbal volley across the bows sooner rather than later. I'm starting to question my own beliefs? I want to see the club do well, but do I trust the men in charge? Will any amount of protesting make any difference? Is it not simply a case of better the devil you know and trying to make this work with Mike Ashley And Co?

After a restless night I have texted Sky Sports pundit David Craig asking if he will set up a meeting with myself and life president Malcolm Dix to chew the fat.

Wardley Legion
What's in a name?

The Villa fresh from there free week last Sunday were back in action today

Just to keep up with that stupid professional football club down the road The Villa have decided to sell of the naming rights for Grange Villa Park, regardless of the fact we don't own the ground and the council does. The forerunners are 'Hood's Nana Makes A Mighty Fine Chicken Dinner Stadium' or the smaller more controversial name of 'Dog Shit All Over The Pitch Stadium'. Either way Sharpey is warmly rubbing his hands from this financial brain wave.

Slug Marshall was missing from the fold today, now Slug gets a lot of abuse from me in the match reports. 99.9% of the time it's well deserved as in truth he's a bit of a bell end. Not today and fair play to the lad for being missing as he laid a wreath at the local war memorial for Remembrance Sunday.

Well done Slug.

The lads however had to spend 20 minutes removing spent fireworks from the pitch so the game could go ahead. Apparently Hardy got caught last night having a little play with himself while watching Lady Chatterley's Lover he was caught as he left the DVD on pause at the sex scene until his missus woke in the night to find him. Thunder Mitchell back watching on the side lines got wrong of his Dad Ken for going out last night and leaving the bath running. Thunder's reply of he was trying to make an indoor swimming pool didn't go down to well. You can tell we are approaching winter as Sir Barrington has started wearing his lasses tights for football. Thankfully they are a nice shade of green to match our strip.

As for the football we lost a highly competitive game 3.2 with the high point of the performance being Boy Whitfield's war cry of 'Come on lads were cooking on gas now' Not sure what this is supposed to mean.

We did manage to lose a ball in a Conifer tree where Thunder Mitchell announced that he was to fat to climb trees to retrieve it. Luckily the aptly named Villa, Ultra Chunky wasn't and managed to rescue the ball so the game could carry on. Chunky is now the Villa's chief tree shaker

By the way Grange Villa WMC.FC play in a park in the Villa.

The name will always be Villa Park.

Traveller's Rest
Horrible

A change in fixture from our advertised Bob Curry Cup game against North Biddick. Apparently they are playing Costa Rica in a World Cup Qualifier. Instead our fixture from December against them plucky fighters from The Travellers Rest was brought forward to fill the void.

Boy Whitfield fell asleep last Saturday night in a bar

leaning against a fruit machine as somebody was playing on it. He didn't seem to mind the chinking of pound coins or the dazzling flashing lights at all. Last night he managed to fall asleep again in a bar thankfully in a chair this time. He was bundled into a taxi at 11.30pm and sent home with a £5.00 note tucked into his back pocket for the fare. If he'd just managed to fall asleep a smidge earlier he might have been able to last longer than 70mins he played of today's game.

However Villa Ultra Chunky didn't have to rescue any footballs stuck in trees this week but I wish the ball did get stuck somewhere it could never be retrieved maybe in Bone Crusher Bob's garden, as we were utterly horrible and crashed to a horrible, horrible 5.2 defeat.

Washington Highwayman
Biscuit

We travelled to a place called Pickle Tree Lane this morning to face Washington Highwayman who stumped us 5.3 earlier on in the season. This was however was the last time Scruffy Haley was seen in a Villa shirt after he was wrestled to the ground by Big George the farting bear (the former Stanley League referee)

Sometimes you wonder why you do it

Why struggle out of a nice warm bed at stupid o'clock in the morning to go to football with a stinking hangover that just won't lift.

What has Grange Villa done for me?

I will tell you -

Damaged ankle ligaments (on at least 3 occasions), a chipped tooth, a lump the size of a 5p coin on my left bollock, mucky cut knees, grass burns and countless thousands of hours filling in team sheets and sweeping out changing room floors.

Is it worth it?

It is on days like this

After a good few weeks of indifferent results we finally grabbed a win in an entertaining 3.2 victory

A morning that started off with no changing room for The Villa and a swapping of pitch before kickoff it was just another confusing, confusing muddled Sunday morning in The Gateshead 1st Division. After a full week of torrential rain the pitch resembled a ploughed farmer's field.

Stupid Ben asked 'who are we playing today?'

'Washington Highwayman' I replied.

'I thought they played in Washington?' he said.

'We are in Washington' was my response.

Maybe he did have a point as our pitch was as far away from the changing rooms as you could go. If we'd gone a bit further we would have been back home in Chester Le Street.

Slug Marshall was back after a couple of week's absence with a new hair style its fluffy and soft like a new born baby's. Hood complained about the clart's around the pitch. But if you're going to turn up for football in your lass's high heel shoes you're going to get your feet wet and muddy. I don't think Mrs Hood is going to be too happy this afternoon.

Sharpey got a bad injury that needed emergency treatment; he managed to poke his eye out with the linesman's flag.

Congratulations must go to young Music Hall who's finally found a job; he's a gardener on an oil rig.

The goal of the game came from the ex Scottish Centre Forward Chrisy P who scored a 300yard screamer just like

Ally McCoist used to do for Rangers back in the day.

The comment of the day was from Hardy when a Highwayman defender called him a fat pig. His retort was so sharp and as quick as a flash 'the reason I'm fat for is every time I fuck your mother she gives me a biscuit'. To be fair to the lad from The Highwayman he did shoot back with a Custard Cream reply.

The not so sporting person of the day was Dog Tit's back in the club who complained like a girl about the lads not putting their chairs away after a pre match pint. Do you actually want us coming in and spending money?

North Biddick – Bob Curry Cup 2nd Round
Revenge

The Bob Curry Cup is the Gateshead League's equivalent to the FA Cup. It's a cup steeped in tradition and history, a chance for the minnows to get a plum tie against one of football's giants, a chance to show the big boy's of the game what we are all about.

Grange Villa struggling in the bottom half of the 1st Division have been pitted against the might of The Premiership's all star side of North Biddick.

Cast your minds back to this year's League AGM where North Biddick's secretary made some sexual references and innuendo's regarding The Villa and some sheep. We sat back and kept quiet, we knew we would have our day, we knew we would have our revenge we would do our talking on the pitch.

The news from our training camp this week in preparation for the big day has unfortunately been a mixed bag – Hardy and Chris Guy announced their absence from the game as they would be nipping over to Liverpool to find a new car stereo with the lads from Pelton Buff's. Young Music

Hall (his dad Albert used to play for the Villa many many moons ago) told us he's packed in his job as a gardener on an oil rig on Monday. Luckily he's got another job as a window cleaner on a submarine. Scratchy Howey announced he was missing today's fixture as he didn't go to bed until 6am as he'd stopped up watching UFC fighting on his iPhone he also managed to smoking 4 boxes of Berkeley Cigarettes. Big DC was yet again missing due to him not realising we had a game on......emm....its Sunday....we play on Sunday's. You thick twat.

Talking about Pelton Buff's yes it was their keeper in a pre-season friendly game some 10 years ago, who kicked me in the bollox when I was through on goal who caused my 5p sized lump that I spoke about last week. Not one of my happiest moments but probably Sharpey's funniest moment at football ever when he ran onto the pitch with the magic sponge to give me treatment. His reply of I'm not putting my hands there while giggling like a girl will live long in the memory.

So this had a heavily depleted Villa side which had to call into action the veteran Clak at left back his first start in over 5 years as well as sub appearances from Fatty Podge and Chubby Singe. A thoroughly wet and miserable morning had the Villa crash 7.0 to far far superior opposition.

Maybe I don't want to talk too much more about the game; maybe we will have our revenge against this lot some other day?

DECEMBER

Cold

Opinion is split between fans over whether we should take the FA Cup seriously this season. I don't think it's our priority. 'Toon Talk's' audience is certainly split with 60-40 in favour of trying to progress to the next round. The various media have started linking players at Newcastle with moves to big clubs in the January window. Nolan back to Bolton? Big Clubs? We are linked with Manchester United's' Tom Cleverly who is a tricky central midfield player who is currently plying his trade at Watford. We face them at the weekend so will get a chance to see him for myself. Glenn Roeder raises his head from under his stone to tell Newcastle United not to be a 'yo yo' club. Thanks Glenn. Now shuffle back off to your stone mate. Just received a great new book today charting the history of North East football entitled 'Pioneers Of The North' by Alan Candlish and Paul Joannou. It gives a great insight into how our club was formed. A must for all Newcastle fans.

I got an invite to a box today so gave up my seat in the Gallowgate to see how the other half live. Went along with Joe Allon and his good lady 'H' and Danny Mitchell from the NSPCC. We were a couple of boxes along from the new Heavyweight Champion of the World David Haye. Nice fella. Well I'm going to say that aren't I, have you seen the size of him! Watford played well today. Cleverley, was indeed clever, and I was impressed by their centre forward Danny Graham who hails from these shores. A goal apiece from Loverkrands and new boy Pancrate sealed the points in front of another bumper crowd, oh happy days. I enjoyed the executive box experience, but it's certainly a lot more subdued.

David Craig rang me today to say that Mike Ashley And Co. will get back to me in due course.

News today that Andy Carroll has had an alleged altercation of some sort in 'Blu Bambu' and has been arrested. Not the best way to celebrate a home win. With the games coming thick and fast I'm not sure we will see him at Coventry on Wednesday.

Just call me 'Mystic Steve'. Carroll not even in the squad tonight, but he is in the stands as we cruised to another 2-0 win. Goals from the fit again Ameobi and Ranger, his first for the club see us extend the gap on the chasing pack. This really is becoming too easy for us isn't it? I'm still waiting for us to fall flat on our face. A seven point lead though is a seven point lead. Chris Hughton deserves credit for this after 7 straight wins since his coronation. Who said the Fizzy Pop League was going to be difficult? Not much about us in the red tops lately either. I wonder why?

Barnsley away at the weekend and once again we have sold our ticket allocation out in record time. An estimated 10,000 Geordies will travel, despite only having 7,000 tickets. It promises to be lively to say the least. Word on the street is that Carroll is likely to play some part in the game as he has trained well. Is that football or boxing? We shall see.

The atmosphere was as expected fantastic. Pity the same couldn't be said for the team. 2 points dropped for me, but they do say if you win your home games and get a point away you won't go far wrong. In fact I said that earlier. Who are they anyway? Nolan again on the score sheet and Harewood who is receiving some stick from certain sections of our support. An interview with Kevin Nolan echoed my sentiments. "It felt like a defeat". Khizanishvili has his last

71

run out in a black and white shirt. He will be back at Blackburn Monday. I don't expect him to darken our doors again. My gaffer was right.

The players have returned from their Christmas party in Dublin with no further arrests so cause for celebration there then. The smoggies and their leader Bernie Slaven are cranking up the pressure and talking out of their arses on the 'The Three Legends'. It's not a bloody derby game man! Having watched a few of the 'Boros games this season and the fact that they now have Strachan in charge I see this game as a formality for us.

More paper talk about Carroll being a target for Stoke and Arsenals' Jack Wilshire coming on loan to us in January. Time will tell. With Khizanishvili leaving and Enrique being our only reliable left back we need to strengthen our defence. If Harewood returns to Villa I agree we will need another forward so maybe Wilshire is the answer. The Beckford story has raised its head again, this time in Leeds, and now Rangers Kriss Boyd is a potential target. Hughton when asked won't confirm or deny any of this, so I guess we will just have to wait and see.

'2-0 we always win 2-0!' Another atrocious game to be fair but who cares. Were the Smoggie fans there? I didn't hear them? Those that did bother to turn up in their transit fan were apparently throwing things at our supporters. Harewood opened the scoring after a blatant foul by Ameobi, much to the dismay of the 'Boro players then Ameobi, who has a great scoring record against 'Boro and the Makems grabbed the second with a bullet header. We have now opened a 10 point gap on West Bromwich Albion and Nottingham Forest. I keep pinching myself to make sure I'm not asleep. I'm still keeping my feet on the ground though. We all know

72

what happened the last time we had a double figure lead at the top of the table don't we. An attendance record was broken in the Fizzy Pop League today with 49,644 coming through the turnstiles.

A boxing day with a difference. A trip to Sheffield and not Wigan for a change. Wednesday not United. Last time we won away from home on Boxing Day was a scrappy 2.1 victory against this lot way back in the relegation season of 1988/89. Pre-match speculation suggested we wouldn't get a drink before the game but fears were allayed by Biffa from nufc.com who texted to suggest a few pubs 6 miles away from Hillsborough. I travelled down with 'Black Sheep Travel' my mates firm and we on the Bud and Becks at 8am. All was going well till we reached RAF Leeming and we were aware of people pointing at our buses wheels. We pulled over and discovered a flat tyre. Fair play to the driver Billy he got on with the job in hand and got his Christmas gear dirty to change the tyre. It wasn't without problems. The jack snapped and he had to flag down another motorist to borrow a screwdriver, but a 40 minute delay wasn't bad under the circumstances. We would have been delayed with extra piss stops anyway. The pre-match boozer was an eye opener. The magpie ranger was there with his mates holding an open mic session. You had to see it to believe it. They had certainly capitalised on the 40 minute delay we had suffered. The match itself was dire. There is definitely a reason for Newcastle United to demand a home game next boxing day against a team that doesn't wear blue and white strips. I thought Nicky Butt was awful. Still I did have the chance to celebrate 2 goals on Boxing Day which is a rare event. A textbook header from Nolan and a great strike by Robs number one Shola giving us the reasons to jump up and down and keep warm in the Siberian temperatures. Much to the dismay of er indoors I watched the game again when I got in and I take it back Nicky! You deserved your man of the match champagne. There were some woeful displays though. Harewood was substituted today and I'll be surprised if he returns as his loan comes to an end. Word leaks out that Chris Hughton gave the players Christmas day off...that explains that performance then.

Derby County under the stewardship of Nigel Clough today and our Rob has turned his dislike from Shola to another player. Step forward Danny Guthrie. 'He contributes nothing at all to the side and can't cross a ball and refuses to stay out wide preferring to come inside looking for the ball', being Rob's argument. On current form I feel inclined to agree, but the lad does prefer to play in the middle so maybe something to address Chris Hughton. Another cracking crowd today, but very quiet at times. I'll put that down to the cold. Not exactly a feast of football today and another bore draw. We created chances but just didn't take them. The unbeaten run goes on, but 2 points out of 6 not quite what we were expecting. As the New Year mince pies are just around the corner I will be taking my first bite and making one big wish that nobody leaves this squad in the transfer window. The squad is still painfully thin and we need a few more in. Sky Sports News and the local papers have us linked with Kilgallon, Robert, Chopra, Beckford, Campbell, Richardson, and a few more. I'll believe it when I see it. I'm still not convinced that Mike Ashley And Co. will release any funds for Hughton. Why break the habit of a lifetime? Happy New Year?

Received a call today from Derek Llambias. He and Mike would like to meet me and Malcolm Dix in 2010. A break through? Peace in our time? As Peter Beardsley would say....'Time will tell.'

Lumley
Father and son

Newcastle v Sunderland that's a derby game (even though both teams are not from the same city). Rangers v Celtic that's a derby game mostly based on some sort of stupid religion. And of course the Manchester and Milan derby's, Grange Villa v Lumley however is as close to a derby game as were going to get in the Gateshead League. It's a bit like them Smog Monsters from Middlesbrough trying to say their games against Newcastle are derby games when they should be slugging it out with Hartlepool. Lumley do however have in their ranks an ex Villa player in the shape of Spice Boy Thompson the heavily tattooed former Low Fell Bouncer just to add extra flare to the fixture.

The thing is he didn't show up for the game today.

And another no show today was the ex Stanley League referee George the Bear who was supposed to unveil the Villa's new goal nets today in a ceremony before the match. He was supposed to be cutting the ribbon across the goal in front of a whole host of dignitary's from the Villa Club's committee. He of course was to do this in full Prison Warden's Uniform and make a speech to thank all his prisoners from Durham jail who have spent thousands of hours sewing the nets together for us.

He was apparently round Tommy The Pop Man's house instead, drinking flat Tizzer.

The day started bad for Singe who thought he'd done a

Speed Y Jelly and lost his wallet. Speed Y Jelly's probably lost about 4 as well as 3 driving licences and a wedding ring in his time at the club. Poor wife of Singe had to find the wallet of Singe back at home then make an emergency trip to The Villa with son of Singe. The Villa were massively struggling to put a side out, it's the sign of the times when a 16 year old boy is your only hope.

Lumley were obviously in a similar position and down to the bones of their squad as well. They may have strips like Brazil's from the 70's but some of The Lumley lads could have been born in the 50's.

The Lumley midfielder who looked like he should have been an extra from The Beano tried to have a fight with Chrisy P; obviously Chrisy P is the best looking lad at the Villa and should never fight this is obviously to maintain his good looks. Thankfully Villa Hardman Boy Whitfield was on hand to sort The Beano Cartoon character out. Podge stood around on the side lines doing a good impression of Dog Tits in an ultra tight figure hugging tee-shirt.

Tinhead pulled the Lumley goalkeepers Amish style beard then scored a penalty this was the start of a Villa goal bonanza as we went goal berserk and smashed Lumley 11.1 with Sir Barrington hitting 4 (in his green tights).

Boy Singe then made his Villa début playing the last 30mins. This makes father Singe happy.

Boy Singe then managed to score hitting in a shot from 7 yards out. This of course makes father Singe very happy.

Singe then made a rare sub appearance to make it the 2nd father son combination ever to play for The Villa following on from Scott and Podge.

Singe then scored after some unselfish play from Chrisy P. This makes Singe ultra happy.

The final whistle went, maybe there was a tear from Singe, I'm man enough to admit it

Whickham Highwayman
Twisty
Following on from last Sunday's no-show of the super stars the excuses came out of the woodwork as to where everybody was. DC said he couldn't play as he's broken his shin pads by dropping a carton of ice cream on them. Well he would have said this if he'd bother his arse and rang one of us up to let us know where he is or what's going on. Hardy was lost in the Gallery's at Washington he spent the morning going up and down on the escalators while munching on a Gregg's corned beef pasty and completely forgot that we had a game on. Young Music Hall was rolling up some of them funny herbal cigarettes at a house Party down Queen Street.

The only one with a proper excuse was Scratchy Howey who was shuttling plebs to The Metro Centre on his Go-Ahead Northern bus as they undertook the joy's of Xmas shopping. He was at the Northern's Christmas party last night at East Stanley Club. All the other drivers for the night's entertainment got to watch UFF fighting on his phone; I bet that was a mint night out.

Maradona Davidson of course is still on the treatment table. Cast your minds back to the end of last season where Maradona caught thrush from Thunder Mitchell's toilet seat during a Villa Ultra house party. Sharpey raided the club's kitty to pay for his emergency treatment at the GUM Clinic and he's never been seen since. If you do see him wandering

77

around the back of Queen Street ask him how he's getting on and find out when he will be able to play down the left for The Villa again?

To be honest it's been a disappointing season so far from the Villa, a season of underachieving and sub standard performances, the race for the Premiership died about September. Other than our twating in the cup game off North Biddick our heaviest defeat and worst performance was an away game back in August to the league leaders Whickham Highwayman. This was the game that had the lads have a big bitch fight at half time as well as a shocking performance from Kebabcop Hutchy where his belly slowed him down and had the Highwayman's centre forward fill his boots. We'd be hoping for a much better result and performance today.

To show how serious we were taking the game most of Saturday Night's Tizzer flavoured fizzy alchopop party crowd stayed in, well apart from Boy Whitfield The Villa hard man. But as his name suggests he's as hard as fuck with a bullet shaped head.
This week was unfortunately a repeat of the last time we played them as we were twatted 5.0 and they played most of the game with 10 men after having a man sent off. They might be top of the league and far far better than us but they would surely win the title for the twistiest team in the league by a country mile.

Sharpey wasn't feeling too well today he put this down to eating a bad Brazil nut last night. He said it was the worst Brazil nut he'd ever ate in his life.
'Why did the drunken chicken cross the road? To get to

78

the other cider'

If this is all Mr Sharpe has to offer I'd rather he didn't bother coming to football and just stayed in the house with his nut crackers.

Villa Ultra Thunder Mitchell was missing last week from the side lines as he's been having 'reach around' sex with a shemale school teacher. He was back this week to tell us all about it in graphic detail.

Chrisy P the best looking lad at the Villa had a pre-match meal of a Scottish Happy Meal from McDonalds. This consists of haggis, Irn Bru and a deep fried Mars Bar. The Highwayman also twisted about dog shit on the pitch. This however I happen to agree with

Winlaton West End (match off)
The Christmas Special

This week we were supposed to play hosts, and entertain them rhubarb slasher's from the high hills of Gateshead's unruly outback. Unfortunately the council in their wisdom called the game off due to the 'slight' weather conditions we had this week.

Actually for this I'm quite thankful, I fear I had way way to much sauce last night and I'm feeling a trifle squiffy this morning.

So that's it 2009 finished on the football front, we now don't have a game until January 10th, where we travel to Washington Steps for more of that crappy, cheesy, pop/line dancing music from the late 90's combined with Sunday morning football.

As I see myself as some sort of fancy Dan artist who's into

photography and writing. Somebody who wears floral shirts and 1970's brown leather jackets. Somebody sadly who's never been very good at sport and in particularly really bad at football I'm going to prove today to you all how versatile I am as a writer and talk about something other than football.

It's something topical and something sadly that I hate.

I'd like to say at this point 'Merry Christmas' to all you lovely readers but I'm not!

Let me give you the facts

Christmas was some Pagan festival that got hijacked, took over and spoiled by a bunch of dippy Christians who tried to brainwash the world about some mumbo jumbo nonsense. Virgins having babies I ask you? That sort of thing might happen regularly down The Avenues at Chester Le Street but I'm positive it would never have gone on in down town Jerusalem way back in 4bc, a lack of a welfare system to sponge off would have stopped Mary bang in her tracks.

This religious festival was then again hijacked in more recent times and completely taken over and dictated to by greedy, commercial and corporate businesses. These companies say what goes on and what society should do, take Santa Claus, for example, he should dress in red as Coca-Cola is apparently lush. Santa Claus was a stupid little German dude who wore green and hid in the trees. Not a dippit fat bloke who a global sugary fizzy pop manufacturer re-created for a marketing ploy.

However regardless of Santa's motives to give toys to children this change was probably a good thing as everybody knows anything red and white is not good.

Its crap, I hate Christmas.

It's a time when you're supposed to be nice to minging twats, mostly members of your own retarded stupid family that you can't stand the sight of for the rest of the year. Uncle Jack and his gammy eye, Cousin Dave and his psychopathic ways, wor Kate and her slip off knickers and collection of lovebites. Each and every one of them to be avoided like the plague, what does Christmas do? Yes put's all the losers of your family together in the same bloody room to argue and bicker with each other.

It's also a time to give and receive tat, vulgar, useless, presents that usually cost an arm and a leg to purchase. Stuff you don't want and will never ever use.

White Christmases are lovely I hear you cry?

Yes if you live in the North Pole and you're a sodding Eskimo, when was the last time it snowed at Christmas? Not for a bloody long time the weather is always crap, wet and grey why don't the zillion poncy Christmas cards you get every year show a crap, wet, grey scene for?

Christmas TV is crap so crap that it drives you out of the house and into the crap, wet and gray weather to seek comfort in your local pub.

However the boozers are always full of good time Charlie's, gobshites and folk who can't handle their bottles of sodden blue colored alchopops. These people never actually go out during the rest of the year they just pop up over the festive period then they get mortal drunk and start a fight. Just to add more annoyance to the season of goodwill to all mankind the price of a pint usually goes up by about 70% and the frigging boozer you always drink every weekend in has the neck to operate a cover charge just to get in the bloody place. Greedy money grabbing bastards.

Christmas pudding is awful, billions of turkey's die, trees get cut down, kids get their hands blown up by cheep crackers imported from Taiwan. Your next door neighbour has his entire house covered in vulgar, tacky, flashing decorations and blow up Santa Clauses to annoy you further and stop you from getting to sleep on a night.

It's all bad, bad; bad wake me up when it's all over.

By the way don't get me started on New Year's Eve and all the twaddle that goes with that! Have a house party and invite The Villa Ultras and then you will see what I'm on about. How much mess and how much drink a group of lads can drink in an hour is outstanding. No matter how much tidying up you do after the party your still going to have hot rock burns in your three piece suite.

That's me done rant over see you all in January probably around about the time when your credit card bill hits the doormat.

JANUARY

Geremi has gone

Hope you all had a good one and have made a good start with your resolutions. Mine is to put weight on, be a miser with my cash and grow my hair. Yeah I'm going to be a Mike Ashley lookalike. Wonder if I'll get much work? Joking aside The FA Cup is upon us and an easy trip to Plymouth Argyle. John Carver is assistant at Plymouth now and he is wasted there. He should be at Newcastle United, and I'm convinced we will see him back at St James one day as part of the Shearer team. There are arguments for and against our FA Cup campaign. I'd rather see us go out early to protect our thin squad, but it's against my principles to want Newcastle United to get beaten. It's a catch 22 situation which I'm sure you have been in as well. Mike Ashley and Co's promise of another £20 million cash injection last year was I'm sure pie in the sky. It certainly wasn't earmarked for players and if we get a few players injured, our 50 points will go towards keeping us in with a shout of a play-off place. Sounds crazy but it wouldn't be the first Newcastle team to be leading a League at Christmas and fall like a proverbial stone in the second half of the season. We have to remember it's a marathon not a sprint. I didn't travel today. Instead I re-enacted the 'Shearer' glory days with my daughter and a beach ball in the living room. She has a great right foot for a three year old and comes off her line as regularly as 'Pav'. I opted to listen to 'BBC Radio Newcastle' and the dulcet tones of Mick Lowes and the reliable John Anderson. The game sounded dreadful and although I hate missing games, found a satisfaction that I hadn't travelled to Plymouth and spent 14 hours of my life on the motorways especially with temperatures dropping in some places to -15, and that isn't a typo! A 0-0 draw and a replay in 11 days time. Well at least we are in the hat for the next round. Why do we say hat? Was the cup draw originally done from a large hat? Discuss. Alan Smith substituted with what 'Ando' reckons could be a cheekbone injury, and nufc.com says he limped off. Watch this space, but if we lose 'Smithy' I think we could be in trouble. Biggest shock of the round sees 'dirty' Leeds beat Man Ure 1-0 with potential Newcastle target Jermaine Beckford grabbing the only goal of the game. The Makems are through beating non-league Barrow 3-0 at The Stadium Of Light in front of 25,000. Barrow bring 7000 so do the maths. The Smoggies fall at the first hurdle again losing to Manchester City 1-0. The cup draw takes place live on ITV 1 with Frank Skinner and Paul Elliot pulling the balls out of a large bowl. Not a hat in sight!? We draw West Brom away much to the delight of Baggie Skinner. I want to beat Plymouth and West Brom...bang goes my concentrate on the league and get knocked out of the cup thoughts. Win those two games and we will be dreaming of a League and Cup Double!

Er Indoors- "Steve....Steve.....wake up...wake up....your dinners ready"

Former Scottish International Willie Donachie has joined our Academy, replacing Richard Money. Geremi has gone! And with him 60k a week off the wage bill. Turkish side Ankaragucu have released footage of him being unveiled in front of their fans. If only they knew!

Two feet of snow at my front door, and snowmen making a comeback up and down the country. Worst weather since 1981 they reckon. Geremi is back! Well in a manner of speaking. He's now gone to the African Nations with Cameroon for a month in the sun whilst we all shiver and freeze, safe in the knowledge that he is still banking 60k a week from Mike Ashley and Co. The Turks thought he was there player but it seems that they were a little premature with their ticker tape welcome for the slowest midfield player in the world. Meanwhile Matthew Kilgallon has declared that he is quite happy at Sheffield United thank you very much and has no intention of leaving a side chasing promotion? Jermaine Beckford puts in a transfer request, with the media circulating a story that Newcastle won't budge from their valuation of the player which is £1.5m whilst 'dirty' Leeds are holding out for £2m. What's £500k between friends man?

The snow which was welcome at Christmas is now getting on everybody's wick. Football matches postponed days in advance as we lead up to the weekend. The country is at a standstill. Our game at Reading looking less likely by the hour. Another snowman has appeared in my street.

Our game is called off. Only 10 'real' games survive the big freeze, and you have to take your hat off to Jeff Stelling on Sky Sports Soccer Saturday who, along with his motley panel make it seem as if it's a full programme of fixtures with their coverage of the likes of Leeds v Wycombe. It finished 1-1 if you're interested. Our new number '9' Beckford played but didn't notch, unlike my daughter who volleyed the beach ball past me into the makeshift goal in our living room. She has got a great right foot by the way. At 3 years old hasn't quite grasped the offside rule yet though.

A glance through the weekend papers delivers good and bad news. Joey Barton is still injured and will not be considered fit until at least February. Collocini has pledged his future to us. Even if Real Madrid come in for him! He has obviously just discovered the 'real ale' bars in Newcastle! Join 'CAMRA' to Colo! You know it makes sense. We are also linked with more players as the transfer window enters its second week. This week's name is Rickie Lambert. A striker from Southampton who has been hitting the back of the net on a regular basis. Hughton says there is nothing in it. We will just have to wait and see.

I've helped organise a charity boxing match at the 'Lancastrian Suite' today and 9 of the first team popped down to show their support. Take a bow Steve Harper, Tim Krul, Jose Enrique, Steven Taylor, Ryan Taylor, Alan Smith, Shola

Ameobi, Andy Carroll, Kevin Nolan and Reserve team coach Alan Thompson. Joey bought an Alan Shearer framed shirt for £2k in the auction. Cue that song! 'Isn't it ironic...don't ya think?'Fair play to him though. A lot of money raised today for various charities. I had a good chat with Alan Smith. I've met him a few times and he is one of the most focussed, committed and honest players I have met in all my time following the club. I just wish he had played for us earlier in his career. Good to see them out as a squad. It's good for any team to play together both on and off the pitch. I left the event today feeling Newcastle United could beat anybody again. Thanks Alan!

With the Reading game postponed Hughton has admitted to the media today that he has been forced into a 're-think' regarding team selection. He was going to play a weaker team but has decided to go for it! The players are making it quite clear to that they want a cup run with both Shola and Simpson saying that they would love a league and cup double. Wouldn't we all. Might have to settle for that on 'Championship Manager' though with Joe Kinnear at the helm.

Krul replaced Harper in sticks tonight and Butt was in for my pal Smith but other than that it was a strong first eleven tonight and we cruised past Plymouth Argyle 3-0 with Peter Lovenkrands grabbing the headlines with a hat-trick. Special mention to the linesman tonight who must have thought he was officiating a game of 'cups' on the back field, because on at least three occasions he just played the game on when the ball was out of play. Maybe his arm was frozen to his side? Some overzealous stewards and police escorted a few fans out in the Gallowgate corner for standing up. A bit over the top and with only 15,000 braving the arctic conditions we needed all the support we could get. To be fair it could have been double figures tonight. Next up West Bromwich Albion on Monday. The biggest game of the season so far. I'd love to see a full house. Incidentally we are now sponsored by the Government! Well in a manner of speaking we are. The club have announced that Northern Rock have decided to sponsor our shirts again. It's a strange set up. It's a 4 year deal worth between £1.5 and £10 million. The value of the sponsorship depends on our success? Gone are the days of £25 million sponsorship deals handed over to spend on pitch dodging players like Owen.

Certainly our biggest game of the season so far. I didn't feel nervous at all. Probably down to Alan Smiths pep talk at the boxing the other day. We weren't on top form today though and a 2-2 draw was I felt a fair result. West Brom came at us from the off and some awful defending from Danny Simpson on his last appearance as a loan player caused us all sort of problems. It's a good job a contract offer wasn't decided on this game alone or he'd be back to Manchester before you could say 'twisting my melons man'. Peter Lovenkrands was the hero tonight and in more ways than one. His dad passed away after the Plymouth game and after a quick visit to his family he was back at St James to pull on the shirt for our cause. He got his goal, the all important equaliser, and as television replays show as I type this, he had a tear in his eye as he dedicated the goal to his dad. Danny Guthrie grabbed the other goal with a sublime free kick, but this is definitely a case of 2 points dropped. Next up West Brom in the Cup. After tonight's game I'm swinging more towards concentrating on the league and letting the Baggies 'boing boing' into the next round. Yes let's hope they get through to the final. The more distraction for them the better.

Puma announce that they will make our new strips from next season. Debates rage on the various forums about a Newcastle United strip having a black cat on it. We are assured it will be a white puma and not a black scrawny moggy!

Matt Kilgallon has decided to join Sunderland. Hold on a minute! Is this the same Matt Kilgallon who was staying at Sheffield United as he was loyal and didn't want to leave a side that was chasing promotion? He is obviously not of sound mind, and will see the error of his ways that is for sure. The form they are in at the moment he may well end up back where he started! Meanwhile Jermaine Beckford has now withdrawn his transfer request and is happy to stay at Leeds. So that's two of our alleged transfer targets out of the window. I look at my copy of 'The Hitchhikers Guide To The Galaxy.' It says 'Don't Panic.' It's hard not to. On a good note, we have signed Danny Simpson from Manchester United. He is now injured though and will miss the next couple of games. The Times newspaper is also running a story about Steven Taylor saying that his season could be over after taking a knock against West Brom. Apparently it could be knee ligament damage. No confirmation from the club on this yet, but he has already been withdrawn from the FA Cup squad. Dark days. Nolberto Solano trumpets a distress message to St James as he searches for a new club. Word on the street is that he will be given a chance to prove himself.

The Hawthorns for the second time this season and another minute of respect before kick-off, this time for the people of Haiti who have just suffered one of the worst earthquakes in their history. West Brom named an unchanged side whilst we made 5 changes, most enforced I would say. We were awful, with the exception of Carroll and Enrique it was a bad day at the office for one and all. Special mention to referee James Linnington. Officiating his 6th game today. Were his previous 5 games rugby or in the UFC? 2 blatant penalties turned down for us, West Brom given 2 penalties which were for me quite dubious, certainly the Kadar penalty anyway. (Remember I'm biased!). Ryan Taylors challenge, well I've seen them given, but a red card? Ridiculous. Tim Krul will have had back ache tonight compared to previous performances as we tumbled out of the Cup 4-2. Carroll has been suffering a bit of a goal drought but his brace today will have done wonders for his confidence. Two great strikes, a silver lining at the end of a dark rainbow. We didn't want to go to Wembley anyway.

Jermaine Beckford scores a double against Spurs in the Cup and another million goes on his fee. Not that we are bothered. Hughton confirms that he was going to recall both Harewood and Kishnavilli on loan till the end of the season. Harewood has broken his foot in a training ground accident at Villa and Kishnavilli has gone to Reading on loan till the end of the season. That will be that then. West Brom draw Reading away in the Cup. Come on you Baggies! Mike Williamson, who sounds like your Bank manager is our latest target. We are also running the rule over James Perch from Nottingham Forest. Both defenders. Still no news on Steven Taylor. It doesn't look good.

Mike Williamson deal is as good as done. At least we have cover if Taylor is injured.

Mike Williamson may not be coming as Portsmouth want more money from us as they have to pay Watford some money?

Mike Williamson, Mike Williamson, Mike Williamson. Who is this guy? 15 years ago we were bringing in Tino

Asprilla in January. How times change.

Mike Williamson still hasn't arrived and Forest not interested in getting peanuts for Perch.

We have signed young journeyman Wayne Routledge from QPR. He's a tricky right winger with a bit of pace. Sounds nothing like Mike Williamson. In all seriousness this one is a bit of a bolt from the blue, but a welcome one. The Chronicle reports that Hughton is now going all out for a striker. Everton's James Vaughn the latest player to be linked. We face Crystal Palace next with a defensive crisis. Ryan Taylor suspended and Danny Simpson injured means we have no recognised right back. All sorts of theories about what Hughton will do. Me? I'd play three at the back and play Gutierrez as one of the right backs. His work rate is good and I think he would do a good job in there. But...I don't get paid to make those decisions!

Cue ticker tape welcome! Mike Williamson arrives in the nick of time to face Crystal Palace who have gone into administration. Neil Warnock is one of my favourite managers. He is in the mould of Cloughy, and not afraid to give you a piece of his mind young man. He must be foaming today as the administrator pulls Victor Moses out of his squad as he is the most valuable asset! Shaun Derry's own goal after twenty minutes won't have gone down well either. Nile Ranger sealed the win for us tonight in the final minutes. I like this lad. Think he will be a real star in the next few years. Routledge did enough to impress in his run out and Mike Williamson looked cool as a cucumber under pressure but there are bigger tests to come. A win and three points, but at what cost? Jose Enrique has been our best player by far this season and you could have heard a pin drop tonight when the Spanish maestro pulled up clutching his hamstring. I'm not a doctor but it didn't look as bad as it could have. It still means 3-4 weeks without a left back without any obvious cover.

Chris Hughton has acted quickly to ease our defensive worries. Fitz Hall comes in on loan from QPR with the hilarious nickname 'One Size'...see what they are doing there? 'One Size Fitz Hall' ha ha ha zzzz. He's here till the end of the season. We have also brought in Patrick Van Aanholt on a month's loan from Chelsea. Lee Ryder in the Chronicle opts for a Dennis Wise look at the pair on the papers website via YouTube. To be fair I'm delighted that we have secured these two signatures and there is promise of a forward to come as we are linked with Victor Moses who may well still get a chance to have a run out at St James yet. Solano meanwhile has signed for Leicester and is expected to face us at the Walkers crisp bowl this weekend. The injury list continues to grow with Shola Ameobi sidelined again. Joey Barton is back in training though and Ryan Taylor will be available for selection this weekend.

Michael Chopra in the news for an incident with a fan on Wednesday. Apparently a fan asked to have his photo taken with him, but then started videoing him on his phone and asked him what it was like to play for Sunderland before spitting in his face? Chopra allegedly punched the guy before stewards intervened. No arrests or charges made on either side. Wait till the video appears on YouTube. Reports that various councils are backing the NUST in their bid to take over the club.

Great way to end the month. Geremi has now left the building! No really he has...no false alarms this time. Good luck to his new club Ankaragucu, they will need it. He is handed the number 75 shirt and Hughton says, "We did not want to get rid of anybody but it was different with Geremi as he has not appeared in too many games and he has a World Cup coming up."

Reading between the lines I think he meant, "He was shit and getting paid too much."

Another point gained on the road at the Walkers crisp bowl in a 0-0 draw. Leicester played most of this game with ten men and many of our travelling fans spent this game moaning. There is an air of despondency growing amongst the rank and file, yet I feel like East 17!? 'Everything's gonna be alright!" Great to see Nobby today, and you just wonder if it might have been worth taking a punt on the little genius.

The Steps (match off)
Its snow joke about the axes in London
With the pitches of the North East covered in snow for something like the last 25 days it was no wonder that our game against cheesy pop line dancing music makers Steps went the journey. Jason the secretary from the Steps did suggest that we have a snowball fight to decide the outcome and to who can claim the 3 points. We turned this offer down due to the expense of having to purchasing 11 pairs of gloves.

Obviously not having a game for so long I would imagine the next time the squad get together outside the club we will all be looking like big fat, rusty pigs. And some of us may even be fatter and rustier than that I'm afraid.

There was high drama at Tuesday night's league meeting with an illegally filled in team sheet.

'Not again' I hear you cry.

Well this time I can happily say it wasn't me. Our recent Bob Curry Cup twatting of Premier League side North Biddick had them carry out some incorrect form filling in and subsequently they have been booted out of the competition. This of course has the Villa reinstated!

A trip down memory, lane rewind all the way back to January 2002 and we were drawn against the then mighty Stag Inn side in the Bev Haggert Cup. They of course couldn't field a team that day due to server drunkenness and the league awarded the game to us without actually playing.

What happened next?

Well John Rackham only went on and picked up the cup one sunny night at Birtley Town's ground as the Villa won the bloody thing.

The only downside to the fairy tale is North Biddick are appealing against the decision and whoever goes through to the next round has to play Premier League side Belle Vue. I might actually appeal against the decision and say we don't want to play them.

Just a quick update on Sharpey and his little gas pipe fitting gang. They have moved on from West Yorkshire down to the bright lights of London and Stupid Ben got upset as he was told he couldn't take his axe away with him. Now in the Villa it's acceptable to walk down the corner shop in your Walt Disney Winnie the Poo pyjamas, nobody cares or bat's an eye lid. It's also quite acceptable to wander around The Vila dressed like John fucking Rambo from the film 'First Blood'. Take Chris Smith from the club as a shining example, he's often seen knocking about the streets in a camouflage jacket wielding a huge shotgun with a brace of dead rabbits over his shoulder again nobody minds or bats an eye lid. Stupid Ben spends his Saturdays in the woods chopping trees down with his axe wily-nilly without a care in the world again nobody's bothered or bats an eye lid.

When Sharpey tried to tell Stupid Ben that the good people of London are different to us and wouldn't understand his love for an 8lb axe he genuinely got upset.

So poor Ben has had to leave his axe in the back yard.

Thomas Wilson
£

Well the bailiffs finally caught up with Sharpey. He was found in Tommy The Pop Man's shed making gibbering and gurgling noises behind a stash of empty cream soda bottles. The top and bottom of it is the Villa are now in a financial meltdown crisis owing money out to the council for the vast sum of _ of a million for pitch fee's.

In this day and age of 'modern' Sunday league football and the increasing cost of pitch fee's, league fee's, insurance, referee's fee's and fines we now have limited funds left in the kitty. No matter how many bingo and domino cards Sharpey sells we still have Maradona Davidson's weekly thrush cream fee's to pay out.

What's next?

Financial administration?

Even the little old woman who washes the strips hasn't been paid since the end of September.

Clak was late for football today, he was filling his van up with diesel and a woman actually gave birth in the adjacent car on the garage forecourt. Now Clak is not known for his human kindness but he rushed to the woman's assistance and helped with the birth. The new proud parent delighted with Clak offered to name her baby after him; Clak shrugged his shoulders and insisted the baby should be called after its place of birth. Now Jet could be seen as an urber cool name in some circles it's just a shame it all happened in an Esso garage.

A new year a new start?

Things on the football front are no better from a summer of the high optimism of a promotion push to The Premier League we are now in the depths of a cold winter firmly rooted in the bottom half of a league of stinking mediocrity.

Today's game against The Thomas Wilson had Skipper Brown win the toss and choose to kick off. Sir Barrington knocks the ball forward to Stupid Ben. Stupid Ben lays the ball off down the right to Scratchy Howey. Scratchy Howey boots the ball out for a throw in.

3 seconds of the game gone and we have given away possession of the ball. It's a tactic we have been using for ever. Swap the names of the current players for any from the last 28 years and the outcome is the same. Maybe we should come up with a better game plan?

Thomas Wilson did have a player named High Tower and a Hoody look alike in their side and both were helpless to prevent The Villa's thumping 5.1 triumph.

Some points of note from today -

Is Chris Guy from the former Easter European country of Czechoslovakia? Does he live on a diet of root vegetables?

Boy Whitfield put in a good shift as an emergency left back due to Chrisy P being on international duty for Scotland's Under 29's. Boy put in a few snappy challenges some of them so late they probably happened last year

Did son of Singe get a new soccer flicks and tricks DVD for Christmas?

DC made a rare appearance obviously having recovered from tuberculosis, bronchitis and gout had a shot at goal that actually went backwards.

Scratchy Howey admitted that the famous Dipton bus crash that happened the other week in the snow was his fault. He was scoffing on a bacon butty whilst he was watching UFC on his iphone instead of driving his bus with care and consideration

If anybody has a few coppers lying about and they want to donate then please forward on to

Neill Sharpe
GVWMC.FC
C/O Tommy The Pop Man's shed
Albert Street
Grange Villa
Chester Le Street

Even if it's just to pay of the little old lady who washes the strips.

FEBRUARY

'Hughton, Hughton giz a wave'
You may have noticed reading this that I deliberately avoided a Jim White style transfer window build up at the end of January. I really can't stand all that crap. A dozen reporters freezing their balls off in car parks waiting for a glimpse of a player exchanging brown envelopes with their agent before signing on the dotted line and waxing lyrical about the fans. Anyway we missed out on Victor Moses who went to Wigan? Best of luck son..and speaking of Best...we have signed him. No not Callum! Leon. Yes Leon Best. Coventry City's target

man who has bagged 10 goals this term already. He's not quite the Andy Cole type that a lot of us were expecting, but we will give him our support and hope that he can add to his tally and get us out of this division and back to the promised land of Bolton, Wigan, Hull....why are we bothering again? Good news on the Steven Taylor front, he doesn't need an operation on his knee but still no news on a return date. Rumours abound that Barton could be fit for Swansea game. Watch this space. Our kids cruise into the Quarter Finals of the FA Youth Cup beating West ham at Upton Park 3-0 with Airey and Inman amongst the scorers. This team look good to emulate Gazza and Allons team of 1985. Think I'll get along to the quarter final.

Friday night games are few and far between, but you know what, I really enjoy them. Cardiff were the visitors today and if you had told me at the start of the season that we would take six points of them then I would have laughed at you. A five star performance from the lads tonight and Hughton opted to play all six of his signings. Another Carroll strike and an own goal set us on our way and Carroll put the game out of reach of the Bluebirds with only 15 minutes on the clock. A Peter Lovenkrands brace completed the rout and I bet all those moaners at Leicester are eating their words now. Routledge was the star man with four assists and he really is the type of player that gets you out of your seat.

Calls for Andy Carroll to be the next Number Nine and be a 'dark horse' for the World Cup are a tad premature. I think the lad has what it takes mind I just think that England can wait and that the Number Nine shirt has to be earned, but I think he's the front runner. Chris Hughton agrees with that to as he says exactly what I have just said in the Chronicle tonight. Kazenga Lua Lua is allowed to go on loan to Brighton.

Bloody typical! West Brom go top as Newcastle United live up to their rollercoaster reputation with a 3-0 defeat at Nigel Cloughs' Derby County who are gaining a reputation for beating the big boys. Where the hell did our 10 point lead go? We opted to stick with an unchanged team instead of reverting to the tried and tested 'away day' formula of 4-5-1. Chris Hughton decides to take the lads for a pizza after the game. The last time he did this we had just lost to Scunthorpe and then went on to record a 15 game unbeaten run; let's hope for the same again. Pass the garlic dip someone. Lua Lua tells the Chronicle he's not sure if he will be back to ply his trade at Gallowgate. Don't think that would concern too many people to be honest. He doesn't seem like the finished article. Let's see how he does at Brighton. Ashley Cole injured at Chelski and the Pensioners are making noises about taking Van Aanholt back. Hopefully Jose will be back by then so shouldn't have any worries.

Another trip to Wales and this time the Liberty Stadium. Another packed away end today to witness one of the most one sided games of the season. Swansea will be scratching their heads and wondering how they didn't win this. Television stats suggest 80% possession for Swansea, but it's no good having the ball if you're going to do nowt with it bonny lads. Andy Carroll snatches a late point again for us with a great header from a great ball by Best.....Leon not George. The kid really is unplayable at times and you just wonder why Shola never manages to do this when he gets his chance. I'm happy with this result to be honest and with two home games on the horizon I'm convinced we can push on and extend our lead at the top of the table now that we have regained our rightful place!

Willie McKay picks my birthday to announce to the Chronicle that Joey Barton will be back before you know it and that he hasn't had a setback.

"He's had no setback but he has rushed back before for the team and ended up being injured again. There's no need for him to rush – he said to me he will be back in February at some point and nothing has changed. When he does come back it will be like having a new signing for Newcastle. He's keen to play his part and, with his experience at Premier League level, he can be a real asset to Newcastle in the run-in. Joey loves Newcastle and he is desperate to play a part in taking them back to the top."

Coventry City at home tonight and another crowd just short of 40,000 although I have to be honest where I sit in the Gallowgate it looked a lot less. An early setback for us tonight as Morrison put the Sky Blues ahead on the half hour mark. A few pre-match birthday pints meant that I had to commit the cardinal sin of abandoning the game for a couple of minutes to go for a piss. A word of warning. If you sit near me then don't go when I go! I always miss a bloody goal. I just turned the corner to the stairs after my visit to see Routledge score the equaliser. Great goal. Just wish I'd been there to see it. The half-time hip flask helped me forget! The second half was a bit of a blur to be honest but Carroll, Lovenkrands, and Taylor sent us all home happy with three points and with another home game against Preston on Saturday we have a chance to increase our lead at the top of the table. Special mention to Danny Guthrie tonight. As you know he's not my brothers favourite player, but the boy done good tonight in that central midfield role.

Chris Hughton comes out in the Chronicle and says that he has a good relationship with Mike Ashley and Co. You know I had almost forgotten about Mike Ashley and Co. They have been so quiet over recent months that they haven't even warranted a mention in these pages. Whether this is a conscious effort on their behalf or not I'm not sure but it's certainly working. Newcastle United fans don't do apathy very well, and the anti-Ashley songs are starting to peter out and be replaced with the 'Chris Hughton's Black And White Army' songs. Not a bad thing. Let's face it we are stuck with Mike Ashley and Co. so we can either rant and rave until we burst a few blood vessels, or we can learn to live in harmony. Well ok, put up with Mike Ashley and Co. When you look at what's happening at Portsmouth you have to be thankful for small mercy's. They are days from administration. It could have been us that you know. Mike Ashley And Co. are at least putting money in and not taking it out. Still no meeting with them as yet though. I'll keep you all posted.

All the pre-match talk today was of Preston North Ends 'The Beast' Jon Parkin. A 14 stone centre forward who hasn't had the best of times recently. His bad times continued today with a below par Newcastle cruising to a 3-0 win. Lovenkrands fluke opened the scoring within five minutes and Preston looked defeated. Darren Ferguson must be sick of the sight of St James. With any luck he won't have to visit us next season. Nolan got back on the score sheet after a barren spell and our last minute link up specialists Ryan Taylor and Pancake sealed the win for the second game in a row. 45,000 through the turnstiles today and a cracking atmosphere. Highlight of the day has to be the crowd asking Chris Hughton to give him a wave, only for him to blank us for a couple of minutes. Kit man Ray Thompson had to point it out to Hughton what the crowd were singing, before he gave us a wave. No matter what happens to us as a club we should always remember that Hughton and Colin Calderwood stood up for themselves, the players and our club when we most needed somebody to. Thank you. At home we remain unbeaten. St James Park is a bastion of invincibility. We have scored the most goals and have the meanest back four. On our travels we are difficult to beat...early season premonitions of further demise seem like a lifetime ago...forget the Walkers Crisp Bowl next season...Anfield here we come. Next up the hornets...Watford away. I'm buzzing....

The FA Youth Cup has a special place in our hearts if you're of a certain age. 1985 saw a certain Paul Gascoigne, Joe Allon, Paul Stephenson and the rest lift a piece of silverware that saw our youth policy finally produce a few rising stars. Ok so we didn't go on to win countless trophies like Man Ures lot but we gave English football Gazza. Still one of the greatest players in the World at his peak. I was guest of the club tonight at the FA Youth Cup Quarter final against Crystal Palace and met up with Derek Llambias after a call confirmed our meeting a couple of days ago. No Mike Ashley but Derek would do. I attended the game with Life Vice President Malcolm Dix and we chewed the fat with a man who has been lambasted by one and all since his arrival. Yes I have slagged the guy off to and in my opinion rightly so. I like to judge people for myself though, and I found Derek to be quite open, honest and amiable. I'm not going to go into what we discussed. It wouldn't be right, but needless to say that he restored my faith in the Mike Ashley And Co. regime. Some of you may think I have been sold a load of flannel, but only time will tell. I had a similar meeting with other supporters last season with Chris Mort and found him too good to be true. As Peter Beardsley used to say, 'Time will tell.' Chris Hughton was there to tonight with a handful of the first team, and I congratulated him on a job well done so far. I asked him if he was enjoying it? His response. "I am, but the job isn't finished yet." Nice fella, quite and gets on with the job, but they say it's the quiet ones you have to watch out for. The fog poured into St James, and we were all bloody freezing but a healthy crowd of 1,291 saw us run out 4-2 winners with goals from Newton, Adjei, Airey, and Sammy Ameobi. Let's hope that the public turn out in force for the semi-final. These boys are our future. Andy Carroll back in Court today for alleged assault in a Bigg Market Nightclub. Definitely going to Crown Court this, and adjourned till April. Let's hope he's not doing pre-season with Durham Jails team.

Watford away today and another blast from the past. Vicarage Road. Feels like an eternity since we were last here, was it really only a couple of years ago? Our record isn't too bad here to be fair and we got off to the proverbial flyer once again with Coloccini stooping in to head home in the third minute, cue bedlam amongst the travelling support. Carroll put his troubles behind him with another well taken header in the second half and helps us grab our first win on the road for a couple of months. Five Live confirmed that our nearest and dearest West Brom and the tricky trees Forest had swapped places, with the Baggies winning 3-1 at home against Derby, but Leicester exacting revenge for an early season 5-1 reversal stuck three past Forest without reply. Current state of play sees us top of the pile six points clear of West Brom in second level on games, and now eight points clear of Forest in third with a game in hand and a far superior goal difference. A home game to come now against Barnsley and another slip from Forest could see some of us tentatively checking out the price of champagne in Costco.

Lumley

Beard

Poor Speed Y Jelly got hit by a bus on the way to Friday nights Newcastle game (it was nothing to do with Scratchy Howey this time) thankfully he was fit enough to play today. It takes more than a bus to stop this lad.

Most of the snow has finally gone so we could actually get a game today; however the kick off against Lumley was delayed for a good 10minutes due to nobody having the sense to actually bring a football to play with.

A vital ingredient needed.

The Lumley keeper had shaved of his fluffy Amish beard since the last time we played each other but Sir Barrington has grown a little grey one in the mean time, his brother Marc also has a nice new backward bouffant hair style on show.

Podge asked the following question what's brown and sticky? The answer is of course a stick.

As for the game itself the Villa came out easy 7.1 winners against a piss poor side on a bog of a pitch with Chrisy P getting the goal of the game. Remember Chrisy P used to play up front for Scotland until Mark Hateley took his position. We will forget the fact that Mark Hateley is English.

Fact of the day Slug Marshal is under 15 stone if he gets on the scales and takes his hat, shoes, coat, trousers, t-shirt, underpants and socks off first.

Singe left the match and didn't go to the club for a post match pint as he was doing stuff with 4 semi nude girls back at the Villa changing rooms...........

The Stella
Valentines Brawl

During the week I somehow managed to ring Thunder Mitchell up instead of Mrs. Singe this in turn somehow got me invited to a Chubba Chub Lolly party at an unnamed house down the Villa were we all...emm...ate Lolly pops. The one good thing from this sugar induced fest was Maradona Davidson was at the party. He's almost recovered from his bout of thrush and should make a full recovery by the time pre season training comes around in the summer. Good news indeed

This morning had George The Bear (former referee and Falkland's veteran) carry out the grand unveiling of his goal nets, there green and white with VILLA in big letters. They're smart as anything, just over 10 weeks late from when we were supposed to get them.

Fireman Scott made the game in the nick of time after returning from his trip to Amsterdam, luckily he didn't get stopped by customs at North Shields.

It's of course Valentine's day which prompted a scrappy bad tempered match that ended in a 1.1 draw. The highlight of the game was a 30 man brawl caused by the normally mild mannered, bouffant hair boy of Marc Ward. Its moments like this when you need Thunder Mitchell on your side with a catapult and a bag of ball bearings. Skipper Brown had to come off with a bad hip injury. I think Sharpey enjoyed giving first aid treatment a little too much.

We also lost another football this one's inside of Bone Crusher Bob's castle.

It's also been announced that Tinhead doesn't want to be known as Tinhead anymore he's now Gav Tav this is in a protest against a high speed Italian train! I prefer Tinhead it suits him.

Greencroft
Hawkwind on the walkman

Our brief revival in the Bob Curry cup came to an end where the league management committee overruled their decision to boot North Biddick out of the cup and reinstate us.

Fair comment as they did bash us 7.0 even though they could possibly be the most arrogant bunch of footballers we have ever encountered.

As for the promotion drive to the Premiership well that dream came to an end around about September time. We have 8 games remaining of a dreadful season and in all honesty we want it to come to an end as soon as possible.

Last weekend's game against The Peartree was called off due to widespread snow again covering Gateshead. This in hindsight was a jolly good move as I was still mashed up on Jägerbomb's from the night before and physically couldn't operate the computers keyboard to type never mind help run a football team.

We played hosts to Greencroft today who are real contenders for promotion. The day didn't start off to well with Boy Whitfield managing to put the brand new VILLA nets on the goal upside down so it read ALLIV and the pitch looked like somebody had rode a tractor around it......probably because somebody actually had.

Slug Marshall announced he was out injured after spending the week trying to get in shape on the Wii fit. Except he's so fat he actually blew the game up and received minor burns to his bum.

As for the game we came away with a 3.2 victory from an entertaining and battling display. If only we had shown this kind of form earlier in the season we wouldn't be humping around in mid table gloom. Even The annoying Greencroft's Max Branning look-a-like couldn't spoil our day.

Former Villa keeper Jimmy D came to watch the game whilst listening to Hawkwind cassettes on his Sony Walkman and using the occasional big words in conversation like 'advisory'.

Thunder Mitchell's aunty Shelly has fallen of a camel in Egypt. We all hope she's okay

MARCH

Barton plays a game

RIP Charlie Crowe who died today. He played in the 1951 FA Cup Final win over Blackpool but wasn't selected the following year against Arsenal. In 1955 he broke his ankle the week prior to the final so again missed out. His legacy lives on with the Charlie Crowe appeal which can be found here. http://www.charliecroweappeal.com/

This may seem a little harsh but I really couldn't help but laugh when the news broke today that Michael Owen will miss the World Cup? Has he sold his television? Is he in solitary in Belmarsh prison? Is he at the Equestrian World Cup with Jordan? No he's injured after his goal scoring cameo in the League Cup Final. The money grabbing horse fancier wasn't going to South Africa anyway?! Owen has boiled my piss all season with his off the cuff comments about being at a club that cares, and playing with better players. I might be a tad paranoid but he has been having a go at us all season hasn't he. If only Andy Carroll had had a go at him instead of Nzogbia.

Still no sign of Joey Barton.

The Club announce a season ticket price freeze. Great idea to be fair and the deadline is 31st March. If you don't pay by then your ticket will cost you the same as it did the season we got relegated. Good strategy to get money in early doors. Let's just hope it gets spent on a few new faces in the summer! Patrick Van Aanholt returns to Chelsea. He played his part. Good luck to him. Just hope Jose is ok for a quick return to fist team action and can last the rest of the season.

Bloody Sky Television never ceases to amaze me! They have just moved the Plymouth game...yes that game with an 820 mile round trip from its proposed Saturday berth to a Monday evening. Forget about the poor bastards who have booked flights, hotels, buses...they aren't important man. Just make sure Don Goodman and Co. are happy. By the way am I the only person who finds Goodman and Beagrie boring on The Fizzy Pop League coverage.

I ended up getting a ticket for the Barnsley game right next to the away fans all the way up in the gods at level 7 for this one as my dad wanted my ticket for an old mate up visiting. Well to say this areas rough is an understatement a hark back to the golden olden days. Some Dean Windass's grandfather look-a-like Barnsley fan went berserk and rightly so he got biffed on the head by a pound coin. Moments later I got hit on the shoulder with a 1p piece. You could tell our opponents were tight fisted Yorkshire men. We throw pounds and they lob pennies back at us. The last time I got hit by a coin was at the old Ayrsome Park ground for a Zenith Data Systems Cup semi final (whoooo). It clonked me right on the top of the head and it fucking nacked. The opponents that day were Middlesbrough of course. Is this a bad omen for next week's Tees/Tyne derby? Anyway the game was the most one sided affair that I can remember for a long while. We seem to be making a habit of beasting teams at home and tonight was no exception. Forget the unknown Barnsley player being sent off this was Newcastle at their best. Neat one twos, great approach play and pin point finishing backed once again by nearly 45,000 Geordies in the Fizzy Pop league! I'm going to miss this you know. Guthrie is proving wor kid wrong with some hard working and play making displays in the centre of the park and he deserved more than his two goals and his man of the match champagne by those boys in the Collingwood Insurance box. Well done lads you must have actually watched the game tonight! Lovenkrands continued his excellent form with another brace and a goal apiece from Nolan and Gutierrez. Yes...that isn't a typo! Jonas did indeed notch today and his celebration will go down in history along with Ketsbaia kicking the advertising hoardings, Cole hitting 40 goals in a season and Shearers passing the great Jackie Milburn! The mask that must have more cheese on it than a Dominoes pizza was unveiled and it looked brand new??? Jonas wheeled away towards the Leazes put on the mask and spun imaginary webs as the crowd went wild. Absolutely brilliant.

I got an invite to The Sports Newcastle dinner and me and the good lady shared the table with Lee Ryder and Bob Moncur tonight and we put the world to rights on all things black and white. Mrs Wraith rolled her eyes every now and then but enjoyed her scran anyway. A fair smattering of toon players in attendance both past and present. Obviously Peter Beardsley was there and old 'Bones' Kenny Wharton. Steven Taylor took the top award whilst Brad Inman won the Jackie Milburn trophy. Up and coming young gun Remie Street won the newest award the Jack Hixon trophy which of course was presented by Alan Shearer.

Lee Ryder never misses a trick and the Chronicle next day and the day after carries a couple of Shearer quotes praising the fans for sticking with the club and challenging Carroll to grab the Number Nine shirt with both hands by doing it on and off the park. The former toon idol is spot on as always. He also waxes lyrical about Chris Hughton and emphasises how important the game against 'Boro' coming up will be.

"They are doing great and I don't think you can expect any more. Chris Hughton is doing a magnificent job. And they look like they are going to go up at the first attempt. Then the questions start again, but as I say, nobody can ask any more of them."

And on the derby... "It's just a game you don't want to lose. There's local pride at stake once again. Newcastle will go into the game as favourites and so they should because they've been magnificent this season."

Mike Ashley And Co. fly in via helicopter for training session and then fly out again. Not really a news story yet most papers carry it? Now I've put it in this book. Am I just as bad as all the rest? People in glass houses?? Anyway Jack Charlton has backed us to win the Non Derby.

The Non Derby at the Riverside is an exciting affair to be honest. They actually gave us over 3000 tickets this season. Probably something to do with the fact that nobody really goes there anymore. The policing was horrendous. It's not usually like this down here but after the game we could have had a mini-Hillsborough on our hands. Coppers with batons raised and snarling isn't required with us lot. In fact that kind of behaviour incites bother. The game finished 2-2 and to be fair 'Boro had the upper hand for three quarters of it. We have the luck of Champions though and a cult hero in the making with Andy Carroll. He had a poor game but snatched a late equaliser to grab a point and keep us on course for a swift return to the promised land. It's not pretty but it's effective. Colo limping off doesn't look good and with Mike Williamson suffering some kind of freak injury at home 'surfing' (the net?), we are down to the bare bones again at the back. Let's hope Jose doesn't have a relapse or I may have to take my boots to the Scunthorpe game at St James on Wednesday.

Mike Williamson is out for a month and we still have no idea what he was surfing? Steven Taylor isn't expected to be back till April. Colo a doubt with a dead leg? A dead leg they don't last five minutes man! Fitz Hall ok though and Kadar looks as if he can do a job so no need to get the dubbing on my boots yet. Kevin Nolan is crowned Championship Player Of The Season by 442 magazine. Thought these things were handed out after the last ball was kicked? Hardly a fair competition. Well done all the same. Do the last 10 games get carried over into next year? Strange. Joey Barton interviewed again. Explaining to fans why he stayed at the club. No mention of wages? He is finally set to pull on a shirt tonight for the reserves. Watch this space.

Well Barton had a good run out against Hartlepool last night. They lost 2-0. He missed a penalty by trying to be cocky and chip the keeper. He then comes out with this in the

Chronicle. "No disrespect to the lads who played, but it was not a full stadium where the adrenalin was flowing. Somebody like myself gets up for that." It's a bloody comeback game man Joey. It meant a lot to the other lads no doubt. Let's hope he can regain fitness, zip his gob up and start earning his pay packet. I like the lad but he says a lot and needs to start backing it up with his football.

We owed Scunthorpe one and boy did they get it! I used to travel to away games with a lad from Scunthorpe called Steve Cross. We started up the 'Mighty Quinn' fanzine in the 1990's and he took me round Glanford Park one day. It always amazed me that you could just walk into the place when you felt like it. Have a game on the pitch if you had a ball. I never dreamt that one day we would be playing them at St James in a league game. Sounds arrogant I suppose but we have always been out of there radius as long as I have supported Newcastle. Anyway enough of memory lane. Scunthorpe ruined my holiday earlier in the season and it was great to see this lot tortured at Gallowgate. An early goal from Carroll should have opened the floodgates but we conspired to miss chance after chance before Lovenkrands doubled our advantage. It really should have been 7 or 8 by half-time but we just wasted chance after chance. Carroll grabbed another in the second half and we went home happy. I attended this game as a guest of Honorary Vice President Malcolm Dix. I gave my ticket to my Dad to pass on to one of his mates again. Malcolm has a long history with the club and some great stories to tell. He should write a book! We were within spitting distance of Mike Ashley and Co. tonight but I resisted the temptation to...go over for a chat. Watching him celebrate the goals it is clear he still has a passion for something. Whether it's the football, or the fact that his investment is fast tracking back to he Sky League is open for debate. The apathy and animosity surrounding Mike Ashley And Co. has certainly subsided. If we were to lose our first 10 games in the Premiership however? Still that's for the future. Let's just enjoy the ride for now.

With a big test looming at Bristol City, Chris Hughton screws his loaf on and keeps the punters feet on the ground with a couple of words of wisdom to the ronnie gill.

"We are aware we need to keep our feet on the ground. We have achieved nothing yet, apart from be in a good position. We know about the passion of our fans and the expectations. It is our job to keep feet on the ground." Wise words.

Bristol City have been a tough nut to crack for the big boys at their place and the same applied to us today. They grabbed an early goal and had us at sixes and sevens, whatever that means, and a fantastic strike from the pioneer of fruit gums, Maynard put them two up at the break with our travelling support looking shell-shocked. Murmurings of discontent are never far away from our lot but to be fair we had good reason today. In the back of my mind though I still thought that lady luck would come good for us. We have had the luck of Man Ure this season and sure as eggs are eggs, whatever that means, Jonas gets a gift from their keeper who had played well until this point, and slots the ball in the onion bag, whatever that is to reduce the deficit. Four minutes later and cue pandemonium in the away end with Carroll pouncing to level and embracing the fans invading the pitch. We will probably get a few banning orders for this, but it happens at the 'Pitz' in Sunderland (sorry SOL) every week and nobody says a word. Great comeback, great result, thank you once again lady luck, we love ya!

Toon Talk has done well this season. We are pulling in roughly 1500 listeners a week which includes our downloads on ITUNES and to be fair I've enjoyed doing the show with Gareth Johnson. The ex-pats love it as it keeps them up to date with current events and we have had listeners from USA, Malaysia, New Zealand, Jupiter...the list is endless. Big thanks to www.nufc.com and www.nust.org.uk for the plugs each week. I'm sure with a few more quid put into it by the creator it will become bigger and better. We have been on air when a few big stories have broken already this season and tonight's show was the biggest yet. It started mid-afternoon before the show was on air when I got a text from a mate saying Steven Taylor had been in hospital. I chased it up with a few contacts and it turned out that he had broken his jaw. A few more calls and it turned out that Andy Carroll had been in hospital to with a damaged hand. It didn't take a genius to work that experiment out. Apparatus: 2 hands. 1 Jaw. Experiment to see if two hands can break a jaw. Method: Two hands repeatedly punch jaw till it breaks. Conclusion: Yes the jaw breaks quite easily. We don't know the true story. It is only alleged that this actually happened because nobody actually confirmed or denied it. Maybe Steven will when he can talk again. Watch this space.

Malcolm Dix called me today to say that Sir John Hall has inoperable cancer of the prostate.

The big question before our trip to Doncaster was would Andy Carroll wear 8oz or 10oz gloves. No of course it wasn't. The big question was would he play? The answer was yes he would, and he was wearing a pair of nifty black woollen gloves. In a tight affair United just shaded it and it was that man Carroll who grabbed the headlines for the right reasons with the only goal of the game just short of the hour mark. He really looks the part in this division I just hope he can take this form onto the bigger stage. With another sell out away end the Keepmoat Stadium was rocking tonight and it would take a collapse of monumental status to stop us bouncing back at the first time of asking now. Stop the press! Joey Barton sighted in first team EXCLUSIVE! To a chorus of boos from the home crowd Barton came on as a substitute tonight. Let's hope he can give us something back in our run in. Congratulations tonight to Steve Harper. He has waited in the wings a hell of a long time and it was great to see him pass Pavel Srnicek's clean sheet record tonight that was set in season 92-93. The strikers always tend to get the praise at our club but well done Steve, 19 shut outs and still 8 games left!

Our centre-halves seem to be dropping like flies lately but it looks like Hughton has abandoned the idea of bringing in another loan player. Former favourite Andy O'Brien has been linked in recent days but Hughton has Williamson back now and he has faith in the young lad Kadar, as I reckon we all do after some very impressive showings both in and out of position. The build up to our biggest game of the season is overshadowed by the death of former left winger George Luke who had two spells at the club. RIP. Former Newcastle striker and cult hero David Kelly cranks up the pressure with a volley across the bows prior to the game saying that he thinks Forest can still catch us. Kelly now assistant to Billy Davies at Forest is clearly not well or was on the drink prior to the interview. We'll forgive you David. News from the treatment room is that Enrique will also be fit for the game against the Tricky Trees. I have a good feeling about this. I've been to another boxing event today and Andy Carroll was in attendance. No he wasn't boxing before you ask! I had a good chat with him and I believe him to be honest. I can't divulge the details but he has a story and he's sticking to it. I just hope he can stick it up Forest tomorrow.

Monday night football is a strange one. The weekend is over. Your back at work, then your brain has to cope with a social occasion again. It doesn't add up and never feels right to be honest. I left work at 6pm with one of my business partners Neil Jackson and went to meet up with Chris Knowles and his dad who had my brother and dads tickets for this one. After some scran and a pint we braved the rain. The walk up to the ground was a tense one and due to weather didn't seem to be a lot of people about. Walking up to St James at night is always special though, and the beam of the floodlights is like a beacon to those of us who like to worship all in black and white. I have been confident most of this season, yet tonight I felt really nervous. The ground was still half empty as I took my seat and waited for the teams to come out. Various predictions were circulating in the night air but all I could think of was not losing to be honest. A defeat tonight could see a collapse. One we may not recover from. The teams came out and once the pleasantries were over battle commenced. The atmosphere was great for the opening ten minutes or so, then as Forest carved out a couple of chances and our cauldron of noise became a saucepan of murmurs and groans. The tension wasn't lifted by half-time and to be fair I thought Forest shaded the first half. Hopefully Hughton would be tossing a few tea cups around ala Jim Smith. We came out to the 'Longsands' version of Blaydon races and seemed to up for it. Carroll had taken a knock in the first half and was replaced by Ameobi. There seemed to be a collective groan around the ground. Shola splits opinions. Some think he has the talent, others think he's not worth a light, but the boy done good tonight. A great first time touch

115

and turn and a pinpoint finish burst the bubble of tension and we were 1-0 up and we had a foot back in the Premiership. A nervous twenty minutes followed, but avoiding defeat would have been good enough for me. Stoppage time arrived to the chorus of whistles from the home fans and then a sublime back heel from Shola finds player of the season Jose Enrique who fires in his first goal for the club in 98 appearances and the crowd and players went wild. 2-0 game over and I think we can all safely start planning our promotion parties! 'I'm a Geordie, I'm a Geordie. Going up, Going up! God Bless you Busker! Another clean sheet for Harps tonight as well didn't go unnoticed. 20 and counting.

The bookies have started paying out on Newcastle gaining promotion today. They are never wrong!

Sour grapes from sour face and dour scot Billy Davies at Forest who reckons we need to spend £60m to stay in the Premiership next season. At least that's where we will be mate.

Rumours circulating today that Steven Taylor isn't a popular figure in the dressing room and is set to leave in the summer. I'm a bit disappointed to hear this as I like the lad. Until he comes out and says anything I'll reserve judgement.

Saltwell
Kids

Tuesday nights league meeting was a funny event, the ever so polite bar maid at Stormont Main club taught me some brand new swear words and the management committee got called 'the cast of Last of the Summer Wine' by ex Newcastle Player Joe Allon. This humour obviously tickled the naughty boy's corner (us, Thomas Wilson, The Steps and Lumley) and more than made up for the crap fine the Villa got for a 'late' submission of a team sheet. If you post a team sheet when you say you did and it doesn't get there on time is this my fault or Royal Mail's? It's only a £5 fine but the little old washer woman who does the strips needs paying first as the league seem to have a hobby of bleeding teams dry for the most stupid reasons ever.

Maybe Sharpey is going to have to sell his gold tooth in the summer.

Back to business and the football today, we were at home to high flying Saltwell Social Club who are sitting 2nd in the league. And 2nd place they deserve to be after a 7.0 demolition job on us, well organised, disciplined, fluent football, what more could you ask for from your side. We on the other hand were piss poor and never in the game. Speed Y Jelly possible learnt everything he knows about football from a Vinnie Jones VHS tape.

A big congratulation must go out to Slug Marshall and his wife Anna on the birth of their new son 'Norman' on Wednesday.

Maybe Slug and his Little Plum style (The Red Indian from The Beano) belly can come of its phantom pregnancy. I've made plans for the baby to be a Newcastle supporting, Tory voting and meat eating little fellow by the time he's one. Talking of baby's Sharpey's kids are locked up in a parrot cadge in Bone Crusher Bob's extension. Bone Crusher Bob lives in the nearest house to our pitch and his DIY renovations have turned the place into some sort of mock medieval castle. I guess that's the end of any stray footballs.....maybe

Sharpey's two children as well. Baby's Geoffrey Miller and Terry Ward made an appearance on the sidelines with the rest of The Ultra's. Baby Geoffrey has started shop lifting TV's from Asda and Baby Terry looks like Macaulay Culkin wannabe. It's obviously cool and fashionable to bring your bairns to football on a Sunday

The day was finished off by the entire Villa team watching some scrap men pinch an old fridge from somebody's back garden down Queen Street as Saltwell notched their 7th goal of the game. Saltwell obviously don't have the same distractions as us

I think I'm off to count frozen peas this afternoon, anything other than frigging football.

Leam Lane
Old Man
Well the bloke who opens the changing rooms at Leam Lane managed to get out of bed this morning. Not sure if he's fallen out with his lass or the fact that there was a semi final being played on the other pitch prompted his actions. Either way we were happy in not having to strip off in the street again or worse still have to change in the allotments around the back. Sadly for Hardy the tethered goat was missing this time.

Yesterdays Boro v Newcastle game had Singe, Hood, Skipper Brown and both Old and Young Pyle make the short trip to Smogside (Thunder Mitchell's Mam wouldn't let him go). This had Singe fall down 8 rows of seats when Newcastle got the first goal and then bash hell out of his legs. Disaster was averted when Hood managed to fish him out of the mass of arms and legs. Obviously Singe doesn't play football anymore and he's entitled to go on a 14 hour drink bender, there is no harm at all in that. And the state of his bruised and battered legs is also irrelevant.

10.25am inside the changing rooms and only 10 footballers are on show. No matter how many times Sharpey looks outside the door nobody else is going to turn up. So the fat, slow, old, drunk, injured leg Singe had to play his first 90mins of football since January 2005.

2.0 down inside the first 20mins, playing on the worst pitch in all 26 divisions the referee then shows young Music Hall a red card for dissent. The referee then changes his mind and wants to send Stupid Ben off instead. A Leam Lane player steps forward and said it wasn't Music Hall who made the comment (fair play to him). The referee swore himself scratched his head and re-started the game with a free kick.

Things were not going to plan at all. Singe then burst into the box and took it past the keeper then missed an open goal.......apparently.

I have no knowledge of it as the drink was starting to wear off. Half time couldn't come any quicker for us.

Sharpey obviously sick of his life had no input into team tactics as he was playing 'world cup' with Clak's bairns behind the goal, he then dug up a relic coins. It appears he'd rather do anything than manage us.

2nd half had a Villa fight back with the Wine and Cheese man himself Cluesy grabbing a goal. Speedy Y Jelly nearly killed a Leam Lane player with a 3 week late tackle and Skipper Brown did lots of shouting. A fight back was on the cards. Sir Barrington got a deserved equalizer. There side line made a noise like a bunch of ovulating hens just as Stupid Ben banged in the winner with seconds of the game remaining with a big big get out of jail strike and 3.2 victory. Leam Lane can count themselves very unlucky. And the 8 players who failed to turn up today better be there next week as I've no intention of bloody playing football ever ever again

Wardley Legion
Tinhead

Yesterday had the bizarre event of Singe and Slug Marshall having a tea party on the top of Asda Stanley's roof. There is no truth that The Villa fatty's caused any damage to the structure of the building. George the Ref apparently told The Boy on Friday night in the club that bald heads are clean and hygienic. I personally think bald heads are exactly that bald.

Wardley's changing rooms have been done out since our last visit. The referee's room has even been turned into a kitchen! The kick off was some 20mins late due to the referee not being able to get his scooter started and then insisting on making a brew in the new kitchen. This delay however did give Podge the opportunity to make friends with the lovely and aptly named Nobby, who of course is Wardley's twisty, hard man. The game eventually got underway with Wardley providing the match ball which looked like it was one of them free France 98 World Cup balls that were given out to school kids. It then got lost in the bushes. Apparently Stupid Ben can't wear shin pads with ankle supports on as they hurt his ankles!

Tinhead asked Sharpey if we could have a team building session around his house where we can all play on 'Call of

120

Duty' on the Playstation 3. His Mam will make sandwiches and give us all a glass of Fanta.

Sharpey said no.

However it was Tinhead who grabbed a last minute winner with a bullet of a diving header after coming off the bench to give us a 2.1 victory. Nobby still managed to kick somebody before the referee blew for full time.

If we win all our remaining fixtures and Washington Highwayman lose all there's we could still be promoted to The Premier League in 3rd place... however it's not really going to happen.

The only small crumb of comfort from the season is if we lose all our remaining games and Lumley win all there's we still can't finish in bottom place....whooo.

Thomas Wilson
Wind

The week gone brought the news that journeyman Hardy has left the Villa to re-join Pelton Buffs (for the seventh time). Have boots will travel or in Hardy's case have vodka will turn up for football drunk. Also a training ground bust up had Stupid Ben smash Skipper Brown's Scalextric set, as well as Villa Ultra Thunder Mitchell and Young Pyle bashing each other with Lego blocks. We don't do things by half around here, nothing simple like breaking a team mates jaw and putting him in hospital etc.

This left Chris Wine and Cheese Clues to take over the captaincy of the team for the day. On a positive note the toilet in the changing rooms that has been blocked the last 3 months due to a massive Hardy turd finally flushed due to the input of some sort of chemical Clak pinched from work. However Clak would rather go to a light bulb show than be witness to

121

all his recent hard work.

I have more Nectar Points on my club card this season than the Villa have got and I don't even shop at Sainsbury's. The poor Thomas Wilson have less than that. This has all the hallmarks for a scrappy game!

Not since the days of Rackham sleeping in one morning before a semi final have the Villa suffered with the clocks changing. Sharpey even sent out a text message to everybody last night reminding us of the time change, I mean it's not like this thing doesn't happen twice a year.

Tinhead turned up at 10.26m looking slightly sheepish if not a little lost. Scratchy Howey eventually showed up at 10.28am. His excuse for his lateness was not because he slept in but the fact that his lass brought him down to the game from his house in Consett. I think she must have been driving a golf buggy backwards in a full on head wind. Personally I think Scratchy was talking shite.

The wind was the excuse for a Villa Ultra no-show as well with the support totalling one fan, Chunky the Tree Shaker. The ever reliable Hood only lasted 20mins of the game before he said it was too cold for him. I personally think he wanted to fly his new kite down Chester Park.

Anyway my predictions of a scrappy game were correct with a narrow 2.1 victory for the lads. They were also plenty of scraps going on around the pitch as well. Fireman Scot's Dad thought a Thomas Wilson player should get himself to Specsavers for some silly comment he made. The referee obviously thought the same as he promptly sent him off. The little fat dumpy bloke playing at the back did some winging as well (Slug Marshall did kick him). He then told Sharpey 'I'll see you back at the changing rooms'.

Now this wasn't an idle threat as Sharpey would see him back at the changing rooms, well if the twisty twat wanted his clothes back. The Wilson lads also seemed to have a passion for shirt pulling.

If you want a green shirt that much sign on for next season.

Old Dennis turned up to watch the last part of the game keeping the wind out in a new coat. The coat looked like something that can only be described as the skin of a lurcher dog.

Back at the club Sharpey to his delight found that Club Steward Keith has now got warm milk for sale on draft for a measly 50p a cup. It was needed on a day like today.

APRIL

We're Newcastle and we're gonna win the League

Paul Barron is one of the unsung heroes this year. Our goalkeeping coach has done a great job with Harper, Krul and Forster this season and he is loving it at the club. In a frank interview with the Evening Chronicle's Lee Ryder today he says when asked about gaining promotion.

"It would mean everything to me. From where we were and what people thought might happen . . . we're not even daring think about that yet. We'll just keep going game by game and see what we can do. But of course it would be an awful lot IF we achieve it. We've got a big team here, the ground staff, the masseuses, people who sort out the travel and the food; everybody has got a big part to play and are behind the team. The atmosphere at the training ground has been fantastic. I don't think I've ever come across anything like it."

We have heard about this 'great spirit' all season long, and I've seen it with my own eyes when I've seen the lads out and about. Let's hope it's something that can be retained for many a season to come. With promotion back to the Sky League imminent the chronicle has a bit of a love in the afternoon feel about it this week with a bit of a toon love in from former players. Take a bow Rob Lee, Kevin Sheedy, and Michael Bridges who are all waxing lyrical about all things black and white in the run up to our trip to bottom club Peterborough. It's simple. We win and Forest lose at Bristol City this weekend then we are promoted.

West Bromwich Albion just won't give in. They win 3-0 on Good Friday against play-off hopefuls Leicester. Let's hope Hughton doesn't tinker with the side too much at London Road.

London Road holds some great memories! None better than that Sheedy free-kick in our last promotion campaign! It's a great trip on the train this game. A few cans a few mates and a quick walk from the station through a welcoming city centre and your there. Over 4000 made the trip today and the atmosphere was electric. Hughton had tinkered too much for my liking today. With Barton and Pancrate winging it and Smith and Nolan in the middle there were a few unused and tired legs in there at the kick off. News of an early Bristol goal had a few of our lot jumping up and down, but they were brought back down to earth with a goal from the home side after a mix up between Harper and his back four. It should have been two moments later but as usual we weathered the storm and waited for our female of the season Lady Luck to wink at us and that she did. A flick from Shola put in Jose and his cross was bundled in by Nolan to put us level at the break. The second half was only a couple of minutes old when we won a free-kick outside the box and Joey Barton stepped up to crack one past the keeper and send the travelling hoards into ecstasy. Shola made it 3-1 on the hour with another shank, but who cares they all count. Peterborough pulled one back to make it a nail biting end to the game but we kept our nerve and can now put the champers on ice! Forest grabbing a point at Bristol now means that a win or a draw at home to Sheffield United on Easter Monday will clinch promotion for us in front of a home crowd. I can hardly wait. Hope the Easter bunny brings me a few eggs to celebrate.

A very Happy Easter to us all! Nottingham Forest's failure to beat Cardiff in the teatime kick off meant that we were promoted without kicking a ball today. I sat in the 'Union Rooms' with a pint of real ale with my brother and Neil and his son and we joined in the celebrations with everyone around us. I was delighted but at the same time a little despondent that we hadn't had the chance to do it ourselves in the game. That's what happens when television dictates the kick off times. Bring back 3pm Saturday for all games I say. The journey to the ground was a pleasure. Fans singing and dancing and spewing. These kick off times play havoc with your guts man. We got to the ground in time to see Chris Hughton and the lads warming up for the game and they received a rapturous welcome. No pre-match music from DJ Rob Byron today was welcomed meaning that the atmosphere built up itself, just like the old days. Sheffield United were the visitors for our promotion party and it wasn't going to be easy. As has happened quite often this season we got out of the blocks behind the opposition and fell behind to a goal from Creswell. Once the dust had settled the lads upped the tempo and tested the keeper on more than one occasion. It was round two of Morgan v Carroll and once again the 'Teams Tyson' got the better of the exchanges. On the stroke of half-time Morgan was warned about man-handling Carroll by the referee and he didn't take heed. The resulting corner saw Morgan tug Carroll and the Referee pointed to the spot. 1-1 as Lovenkrands duly despatched the spot-kick. The roof came off all 4 stands I swear! Former midfield maestro Gary Speed was sent off from the dug out for complaining about the decision. The second half was a tight affair as the Tykes made us work hard for the win. Nolan wrapped up the points with a bicycle kick that I have practised for years in the back garden and never been able to perfect. Jammy sod. So a 2-1 win and we are back from where we once came. Job done. Now for the title.

Hughton deserves all the plaudits thrown his way this season as he joins great managers such as Harvey, Cox and Keegan in the promotion hall of fame. His interview in the Chronicle tonight though speaks volumes for the man as he prefers to praise those around him.

"It feels great to join them. I'm so proud and it's a proud moment for my family as well. You're always aware of the fact that there have been a lot of people involved in this. I've worked very closely with Colin Calderwood all season, who has been brilliant for the club, as has (goalkeeping coach) Paul Barron. They have to take a lot of the credit as well. We've had difficult periods when we've not played so well, but we still won our games. We've had to really dig deep to find the spirit. We've kept the competition going all season. That is real testament to the team ethos here."

The media announces that Sir John has cancer. The good news is that he can have treatment, but the fact that the cancer is aggressive sounds serious. I'm sure he will fight it. He did a lot of good for the club and although he made a lot of money as well I'd say his intentions were good and he had a lot more scruples then some others I could mention.

The Young Guns get a credible 1-1 draw at Aston Villa in the semi-final first leg at Villa Park with Phil Airey grabbing the all important goal. Maybe a league and cup double of sorts is in sight after all!

Another chance to gain revenge on one of the few teams to beat us this season Blackpool. They turned up with orange shirts and left with red faces as a master class of finishing from Carroll, Nolan and Routledge backed up another goal from 'Spiderman' who weaved his web again at the Leazes End to leave the Blackpool fans all at sea and choking on the Black and White rock! This team has hit form at the right time and have never looked back. Goals are flowing and the title is within reach. How I hope we lift it in front of Roy Keane.

More stories circulating in the red tops and broadsheets about what we will spend next season. Suddenly the knives are out again from some of the fat boys and girls in the press. A certain Makem lover imparticular licks her lips and salivates as she types her poison into her keyboard. Sad inbred. Still she has to pay the rent as nobody would pay her to spend the night with her.

The players really seemed focussed on the job in hand and

are making all the right noises prior to the Reading game. They want the title, they want 100 points and they want an unbeaten home record. Nolan , Carroll and Lovenkrands all want to finish top scorer. I'm sure there must be a players wager on this. The big question is who will lift the Championship trophy when we win it....not if...Butt as club captain? Smith as Captain? Nolan as Captain? For me it should be Chris Hughton. The bloke deserves the chance to be the hero. He won't like to but he should do it.

The club have announced that there will be no open top bus celebration this year. Personally I'm gutted for the younger fans. I've witnessed previous celebrations; it would have been nice for the bairns.

Reading looked like a potential banana skin to me in the run in but another long trip saw us reap another 3 valuable away points with a Kevin Nolan double meaning he has now scored 18 goals for us this season. A bizarre own goal by Danny Simpson meant that Harper could not add to his impressive haul of shut outs but this win takes us another step closer to winning the title. We now just need a single point from our remaining fixtures to get our hands on the silver urn like pot thingy. This weeks charts now see Lovenkrands at 3 with 15, Carroll at 2 with 17 and top this week Kevin Nolan with 18!

Went to watch the young guns try and emulate the class of '85 tonight but they fell at the final hurdle. I watched the game with Malcolm Dix and Tim Cantell Jones and the bairns lost 1-0 so 2-1 on aggregate. Had they put away the first half chances they would have been taking on Chelsea in the final but it just wasn't to be. The game was played in front of almost 5,000 fans on a Friday night…'Boro' would die for that on a Saturday at 3pm wouldn't they? Caught up briefly with Derek Llambias and Chris Hughton again tonight. Passed on my congratulations to them both. Hughton has a real passion for the job. It seeps through his pores when you shake his hand. I maybe wrong but given a little bit of backing then we may have found a gem amongst all the coal. I hope I'm right. Mike Ashley was here to and he was apparently due to have talks with Hughton about next season according to the media. Also saw Steven Taylor. He still looks in a lot of discomfort. I didn't ask him what had happened. It was fairly obvious. Just hope the issue resolves itself in the coming months and that we can hold onto both players.

The General Election has been called and politicians fall over themselves to back the NUST bid to buy into the club. This is why politicians are slated. Where were they all a few months back when the 'Yes We Can' campaign started?

Shola's shirt from the Sheffield United game signed by all the players is stuck on EBay after falling into NUST's hands and currently stands at £4,500. I bet it's our Rob bidding!

Volcanic Ash grounds all flights and our mammoth trip to Plymouth looks like being a right royal pain in the arse, but it will be worth it if we can clinch the point we need to win that tall slim pot thingymigig.

The Chronicle holds a bit of a 'Toon love in' this week with players praising Hughton and Hughton praising the players. Nothing from Mike Ashley and Co. as yet. Alan

Smith shows his true feelings for the club in another Chronicle interview.

"It will mean as much to me as winning the Premier League at Man United. I've played a big part in what's happened this season. When we were relegated, everyone was seeing it as the world coming to an end. That's how you feel – that there's no light at the end of the tunnel. This season has proved it's a good competitive league. We've respected every team we've played against. I think it's given the city a team to be proud of at the minute."

John Carver quoted in the Chronicle tonight prior to the Coach trip from hell saying that he hopes the lads he worked with Carroll and Ameobi don't comeback to haunt him. Plymouth need to win to have any chance of survival.

A party like atmosphere at Home Park tonight saw Newcastle United win the Fizzy Pop League Title and saw Plymouth relegated. Two first half goals from Andy Carroll and Wayne Routledge after great play from Guthrie and Barton saw us seal the victory we needed to clinch our first piece of silverware...well since the last time we won it in 1993 at Grimsby. This night/game was so reminiscent of that night and the celebrations and pitch invasion were just as good hearted. Plymouth deserve a lot of credit for the way they handled tonight. They unfurled a banner at the start of the game congratulating us on our promotion. At the end of the game the DJ played 'Blaydon Races', 'Local Hero', and 'We are the Champions', if I ever meet him I'll buy him a pint. Not sure if Kevin Nolan had been on the champers early as he spewed his ring twice on the pitch tonight. He was still tremendous. As was Joey Barton in the middle. A sign of things to come I hope. The scenes on Sky tonight of the lads led by Alan Smith and club masseur Mickey Holland shaking bottles of champagne and singing champi-oneys was one to savor. The next time though Mickey...leave your top on lad.

Last nights result is beginning to settle in and just realized my dream will come true. The lads parading the trophy in front of Roy Keane....altogether now...KEANO HE.....

Some great photos in the papers today from last night. Andy Carroll says that the night will live with him forever and that he wants to finish the season in style.

Youngster and fringe first team player Haris Vuckic is been linked with a move to Manchester United today. The 6ft 2inch forward is also an outside bet for a World Cup place for Slovenia. We need to keep a hold of this lad.

Former midfield player Charles N'Zogbia was arrested today on suspicion of getting somebody else to take his driving theory test. What was he thinking? Great news on the injury front for Steven Taylor as he is back in training and is expected to feature in our final game at QPR. Hughton quoted in the Chronicle tonight about his contract saying that it's not a concern at this moment in time and that he was only focused on promotion and winning the title. Having achieved that he now wants to concentrate on assembling a team that can compete in the Sky League.

Derek Llambias breaks Mike Ashley and Co.'s silence at last regarding the clubs return to the Sky League in a Chronicle exclusive.

"Today is a special day for our fans and a big day for Chris and his players. You have packed out St James' on numerous occasions this term and from our very first game of the season down at West Brom, have helped create an unbelievable atmosphere in every game we've played in. That support has undoubtedly rubbed off on the players and go them through some very tough fixtures. I'd like to say a big thank you for your incredible backing this season. It has been a monumental effort from all concerned here at Newcastle United this season, from Chris Hughton and his players and all of our staff at the training ground and here at St James' Park. I'd like to say a huge thank you to everyone at this football club for everything you've done this season. I'm well aware of how difficult things were this time last year and the potential struggles we faced going into this season, but all of your efforts have helped contribute to what has turned out to be a successful campaign. Going back up to the Premier League was always our aim this season and we're delighted that this great club is now back where it belongs in the top flight."

Nicky Butt agreed a few months back to come and do my Sunday league teams presentation and he kept his word and turned up to hand a few dust collectors to the lads. He confirmed that he was hanging up his boots and that he would be lifting the Fizzy Pop League trophy with Alan Smith after the game with Ipswich on Saturday. He left The Swan Pub in Heworth to a chorus of Nicky Nicky Butt. He's been a good servant to the cause.

The final home game of the season is upon us and I make sure that er indoors knows that she won't get much sense out of me this weekend. I met up with my Dad today for a bit of bonding and we put the Black and White world to rights. The sun shone down on us as we walked with a bounce in our step up to the ground. It was heaving as we made our way up the steps to the turnstiles. The Swan's player of the season Dom

Clauzel joined us today as our Rob couldn't make it and as we got to our seats you could feel the carnival like atmosphere. Days like these don't come along very often you just have to enjoy them while you can. My pre-match bet of 5-0 and a Kevin Nolan treble was always going to be highly unlikely but odds of 150/1 swayed me to take the bet. The game was quite entertaining and renditions of the 'Keano' song were loud and proud. Ipswich weren't the pushovers they were earlier in the season and they came to spoil the party but goals from Carroll and a penalty from Shola fittingly won by Nicky Nicky Butt sealed a point in a 2-2 draw with Ipswich grabbing a late equalizer with thirty seconds left. He was a mile offside but who cares. We are up. We are title winners. We are record breakers. Unbeaten at home all season for the first time in 103 years and another attendance record set in the Fizzy Pop League with 52,181 cheering the lads on. The presentation was brilliant and I don't admit having a few tears in my eyes. The team and Chris Hughton deserve to enjoy this moment and it seemed like all 52,181 stayed to pay their respects. I joined up with the lads after the game for a few pints and we managed to blag the party of the year at the Diamond in Ponteland. The team were holding a party to celebrate their success and I got an invite. Everybody was there even Mike Ashley and Co. and special guest was of course the trophy. To hold that in your hands is a very special moment. After all it is the 'proper' trophy. I feel honoured to have been a part of those special celebrations and it is something I will remember for a long time to come. Thanks Kev!

Tayls is struggling for QPR. Pity I'd really like to see him play some part. Jonas won't be traveling to London next week as Hughton has let him leave early so he can prepare for the World Cup.

10373455. No that's not my bank pin code. It is however how many fans we have had through the turnstiles this season. Sunderland managed 719,107. Now who is the biggest club again? Remind me?

Winlaton West End
Doris makes the dinner

Word has filtered through to Camp Villa that I'm not flavour of the month with The Thomas Wilson due to the last match report; apparently the small dumpy bloke with the bad hair is slightly angry about it and wants 'to do me'. Never mind. Also more bad news has reached us with the sad demise of The Easter Bunny. He was shot by Chris Smith and fed to his ferret. Speedy Y Jelly has also had a hand amputated in a freak accident on a roof. Not sure if Baby Geoffrey's machete was used. It looks like he could be out of action for the remainder of the season.

Yesterday morning had me franticly ring around my list of contacts looking for a referee for today's game. Obviously referees are not to numerous in my social circle but I was offered a new plasma screen TV, 18 unused tractor tires and a diamond encrusted Faberge egg in my fruitless search for an official it appears that nobody wanted the job. A big thanks to Happy Harry the league secretary for eventually sorting out a ref as I was chugging on pints in Newcastle before during and after the Blackpool game.

The 'new' referee however held the game up for a good 5 minutes as the Winlaton lads did some complaining about the amount of dog shit on the pitch.

For us at the Villa this is unfortunately something we

134

have just grown to accept. Thankfully Slug Marshal came to Winlaton's rescue with a shit flicking scooping stick he found in the bushes.

More depressingly the team today was yet again another scratched together side with the Villa's tubby back four having a combined weight of 372 tons. Thankfully Boy Whitfield turned up in time to add a bit of youth to the substitute's bench of Clak and Singe. The Boy was late as he'd had a night in Power House with some of his 'special friends'.

Stupid Ben's Mam Doris came to watch the first half and obviously brought some luck as The Villa romped to an early and easy 3.0 lead. Unfortunately Doris had to leave to get the dinner on and whip up a batch of her world famous Yorkshire Puddings. Ben does like a good dinner.

This is when things went wrong, deep in dog shit stoppage time of the first half Winlaton grabbed an equalizer to make it 3.3 at the interval.

After the restart the ball got booted into Bone Crusher Bob's castle then a Winlaton player took a bit of a girly wobbler as we didn't have a spare ball on the line ready for him. Sharpey's quick but honest reply of 'It's fucking Grange Villa, not Aston Villa' however was lost on him. This was about as good as it got on the footballing front as we crumbled to a hefty 7.4 defeat. Fireman Scott got injured near the end and had to be substituted this left Clak and Singe to draw straws to who would replace him. Singe lost and had to play Clak laughed. By this time Sharpey had wandered off back to the changing rooms and didn't want to take any further part in the match. Our final home game of the season came to an end and it's safe to say out of all the players used by Grange Villa this season I would want Marc Wards bouffant hairstyle the least. Even a few of the Winlaton players were laughing at it by the end of the game. Congratulations must go to Scratchy Howey after being Northern Bus's best driver for the second month in a row; he's been given a promotion. He now stands outside the bus depot smoking cigarettes for a living.

My own personal highlight of the day wasn't the annoying Tinhead shouting for offside 342 times but the Winlaton player who tried to stop the ball going out of play for a throw in, he then promptly ran into the golf course fence.

A cat question for the day
It is said that if you chuck a cat off a roof it will always land feet first, would the same rule apply if you added butter to the cats back before you dropped it?

A Grange Villa fact for the day
They are more ears in The Villa than people

Peartree
'Pork Dip'
Sharpey so pissed off with last week's game has left the country!

Well almost.....due to volcanic ash from Iceland grounding all UK air traffic he managed to get as far as Berwick where he's stopping in a caravan with Tommy the Pop Man for the weekend. There must be something a bit chummy in this trip, it's also worth remembering that Tommy the Pop Man has never ever been to watch the Villa in all his life. He has however delivered lots of bottles of pop to lots of people in Chester Le Street.

The biggest shock off the day was Marc Ward and the recent pressure he's been under to get a haircut. Well he's relented and his new hair style looks lush. My next trick is to carry out the same campaign on his brother Sir Barrington. Fireman Scott injured in last week's demolition by Winlaton unfortunately wasn't fit enough to play, this had Boy Whitfield yet again have to play as goalkeeper. It's such a shame we didn't even have a keeper top or any gloves. Well prepared as usual.

Just when we all thought we had seen the last of Hardy he tuned up to watch the game and spent the morning ripping up peoples clothes and eating dead butterfly's. Not to be out done by this former Villa defender Gary Lee also came to watch and spent his morning setting fire to tins of Ralgex deep heat spray and calling the rather tubby looking referee 'pork dip' at every available opportunity.

'Deka' the self styled king of The Peartree's midfield had some big bling diamond ear rings and had the distinction of calling Podge fat. Podge asked him if he fancied a 'belly off' 'Deka' declined the offer and 'Pork Dip' the referee told 'Deka' off for being silly. Gary Lee swore and shouted 'Pork Dip' a few more times and Clak sprayed Danny Hill with the last of the Ralgex. That just about sums the day up as we lost 3.2. Boy Whitfield might look 60 but he can save penalties. Even if we had to borrow some goalkeeping stuff from The Peartree.

Washington Steps
Viva Last Villa

Yesterday the Toon happily paraded around a packed St James Park the Championship trophy, safe in the knowledge of a successful campaign and a well deserved promotion. A job well done.

Singe on the other hand ate a burger from Washington's finest scran van today. It was a time for him to reflect, a time to look back on another season of high optimism and expectations, but yet again a one that ended in mediocrity and underperformance.

At least the greasy burger tasted nice.

Out of the 40 people associated with the Villa how come I'm the only one who hasn't missed a single second of the 32 games we have played?

Dedication or madness?

Well enough is enough today brought the end of my reign as Villa secretary. I'm stepping down from the job with Podge hopefully taking over the Bic Biro and stamp licking duty for next season.

Anyway we travelled away for the same fixture where we started the season with, a game in Washington to take on The Steps and bring the curtain down on the 2009/2010 campaign. Some pheasant shoot in the woods opposite the pitch made the place sound like Beirut as we took to the pitch for a rare game in our blue away strip. The injured Fireman Scott came to watch the game with a new haircut on the advice from Bouffant Ward. It looks like his Dad had done it with the teeth of a Yorkshire Terrier. As mentioned he was still injured and Boy Whitfield yet again had to play in goal. This week he had no such luck in borrowing a pair of keeper gloves and had to do a retro 70's bare hand job. Sir Barrington did offer to borrow him a pair of ski gloves; this offer to our amusement was sadly declined.

He didn't really need gloves as he didn't have much to do as we cruised to an easy 5.2 victory, even young Music Hall got on the score sheet with his first ever goal for The Villa. Main highlights of the game was Chrisy P (the best looking lad at The Villa) getting hit in the wanger of the ball, Skipper Brown getting his nose bust and Tinhead calling DC a donkey. The last 10 minutes of the game had a new record for the fattest centre forward partnership as Podge and Singe went up front, this easily beats the previous combination of Singe and Slug Marshall by some 6 stone. Podge other than being fat and soon to be promoted to secretary of The Villa is the driving theory test manager down Durham. He assures me that nobody could pull a Charles N'Zogbia style scam on his shift.

Our end of season trip to Thirsk Races is booked in for next Saturday followed by a night out in the flesh pit of Hartlepool where it's acceptable to piss on the dance floor of nightclubs........apparently.
Some of the above are true made up stories

MAY

The Chronicle reveal our financial situation.
The club now owes Mike Ashley £111 million.In the event of a sale he must be paid this money back in full.
I've been a good mate with Peter Ramage for years and

having missed out on a ticket for QPR he said he'd get me a couple for the match. Unfortunately they were for the home end in the South African Road stand but it had a posh bar so that was alright then I suppose. I was going down alone and meeting up with my mate Christian at the ground, but bumped into Billy Askew and a few mates at Central Station and shared some pop and some chicken wraps as the trains in and out of London were dry for the day. The Sunday Sun chose to run with the headline 'Mike Ashley Ready To Claim Back £111 million loan'. You then read the story which completely contradicts the headline. It's no wonder I never buy this paper. We got to the 'Central' bar at Shepherds bush and i bumped into a few mates there and managed a couple of pints before the walk up to the ground. The rain had threatened to call the game off, but I'm sure the 'Met' didn't want 3,000 geordies mulling around White city on the drink all day so it got the go ahead. I got to the ground with five minutes to spare but Christian was late and as a result we missed twenty minutes of the game. We got to our seat and although not in colours obviously stuck out like a sore thumb. The game was a non-event and at half-time we headed towards the 'Platinum Lounge' for a quick half-time bottle. I met up with a couple of lads I know in there and Nicky Butt came over for a bit crack to before we headed back up to the stand. This was where the trouble began. An old fella in front of me in his sixties was getting a load of grief off a QPR fan complete with 'stone island' jacket. The QPR fan was in his forties and as high as a kite. It turned out the three men in front were Newcastle fans and our man from QPR was not happy that they had chosen to sit next to him. The combined age of our lads was about 180 so he really was special this nugget. As the bloke became more aggressive another

Newcastle fan came over the chairs behind me to try and calm things down. I bit my lip and said nothing, until our man from QPR decides to start pushing the oldest fella. I couldn't see that so I intervened and told the bloke to sit down and leave it. Daft I know, but I'm sure you would do the same in the same situation. Our discussion became heated which wasn't helped by the fact that Peter Ramage was being sent off at the time. Having had my say I sat down only to see the stewards come up and remove the three old blokes in front of me. Next thing I know our man from QPR is jumping up two rows ala Green Street to have a go at me. Me and Christian were suddenly surrounded by the cast of 'Football Factory' and 'The Firm' rolled into one. Not being a connoisseur of football violence i chose the next best option and crowd surfed to safety and into someone's half-time bovril. The stewards helped me up asking me if I was alright and saying that it wasn't my fault. As I looked back there was a cartoon like melee of hands and fists with the odd stone island badge all hitting themselves. Special mention to the huge gentleman of coloured persuasion who shouted the immortal line 'Come on then you Geordie Bastards!' He'd obviously been watching 'Cass' that morning. The stewards took me to the away end to a welcome of sniggers and polite applause and a chorus of 'He's here , he's there, he flies through the air Stevie Wraith' from a few lads i knew. My head was bleeding at the back from my crash landing but with the amount of people wanting to stove my head in I took that as a result. Christian had made it out alive but was escorted out of the ground. The stewards came up to me wanting me to make a statement but to be honest I didn't really have any grievance. Nobody had managed to clip me because of my 'flying ability' so no harm done. Lovenkrands goal was superb and I decided to call it a day after paying homage to him, as I didn't want to chance my arm with the QPR hoolies after the game. I headed back to Clapham North for a few pints with Christian before coming back on the train with Billy and the boys who couldn't wait to revel in my misfortune. Peter Ramage was full of apologies. His Mam and Dad had been abused to. Next time he has promised me tickets for the away end. Let's hope it's a long time before I have to see QPR again. Had to laugh on my return at some of the message boards laughing at my misfortune. Some people alleging that I was giving someone a kicking before being launched by the big guy. All figments of some very lively imaginations. I'm just glad I got out in one piece to read the comments. So next stop the Premiership. Wigan, Bolton, Stoke. Why are we bothering?

What a difference a year makes eh!

Last May we were wallowing in self pity and wondering where it had all gone wrong. The defeat at Villa Park and the realization that our time was up took a while to sink in. The summer was a long one, but in terms of actual days it was actually shorter with the season kicking off earlier than the Sky League. The pre-season wasn't a bad one with the only shock being the 6-1 humping at Leyton Orient. This was almost certainly the turning point for our season and the players got themselves together in the changing rooms and sorted it out themselves. The money grabbers and time wasters were asked to decide what they wanted to do and they picked up their bags and darkened someone else's door. What we were left with was a team that cared. A team that wanted to prove the doubters wrong. A team that could entertain and a team that could scrap. There have been some great goals and some great games and I really have enjoyed this promotion more than others. Why? Because it wasn't expected. There have been a few blips along the way but over the season we have deserved to win the title. The January transfer window was certainly what the doctor ordered and it boosted our squad which was threadbare to say the least. Wayne Routledge gave us something different and the arrival of Mike Williamson at centre-half was key with Steven Taylor suffering that injury. Kevin Nolan has been inspirational this season and he more than anybody has had a big influence on our success. Steve Harper deserves a special mention as well for the 21 clean sheets he has kept, another club record shattered.

The apathy and animosity that surrounded the club in the summer all but disappeared in the New Year as it became more and more apparent that we were going to bounce back at the first attempt. The NUST was formed and continued to build its membership though and at last we have a credible organization for supporters to join. Toon Talk has also gone from strength to strength to thanks to the support of the Toon army worldwide. So now for the Sky League. Our race to the Premiership is complete and we once again find ourselves dining at footballs top table. Over inflated pints at plastic all seated stadia where the home fans can't sell all their tickets. I can't wait. But seriously, we are back in the big time and I think we have learned a few lessons. We certainly won't take our position in the Premiership for granted, and I'm sure this set of players will work a lot harder than the class of 2008-2009 to retain their position in the league. Who will stay? Who will go? Is Hughton the right man for the job? Will Mike Ashley and Co. sell the club? All questions being bandied about in pubs and clubs in Newcastle as I write. As Peter Beardsley would say, 'Time will tell."

End?

Maradona Davidson never recovered from thrush and was out of action for the entire season

Hardy was never sober, never fit, never fast and never any good

DC missed too many games from eating ice cream and generally was an unreliable twat

There was too much dog shit on the pitch

Too many balls got lost in Bone Crusher Bob's Castle

Sir Barrington spent to long bellowing in the centre circle like the school teacher that he is (he got worse when he started wearing green tights)

Speed Y Jelly didn't kick enough people

Speed Y Jelly kicked too many people

Skipper Brown was often drunk

Tommy the Pop Man looks like Joe Kinnear's dad

Stupid Ben had no shin pads, to small shin pads, to big shin pads, shin pads with ankle supports, shin pads without ankle supports or the wrong boots.

Scratchy Howey spent too long on his iPhone and smoking tabs.

Singe spent most of the season zapped from licking poisonous South American toads

Boy Whitfield was to bald

Slug Marshal escalated in size and girth. Have you ever seen a fatter vegetarian?

Hood said he would turn up to watch then didn't to many times

Thunder Mitchell eventually ran off with the goat that used to be in the allotment gardens at Leam Lane

All of the above are excuses we could use for a very disappointing season of an 7th place finish in The Gateshead and District First Division are irrelevant the truth is the league table doesn't lie and they are 6 teams better than us.

As I previously mentioned I'm standing down as secretary of The Villa, it's a job I reluctantly took on in the first place, a job I've done for 5 seasons. A job at times I've enjoyed but often felt out of my depth and unable to cope with. A job that's often caused me unnecessary hassle and drama. My uttermost respect goes out to anybody who's ever had anything to do with Sunday morning football especially those behind the scenes. Those who raise/collect money, fill in forms, confirm games, ring referees, wash strips and attend league meetings. Those who then get told after all this they are not very good at a job that they do for free.

In all honesty it's a thankless, thankless task.

I'd like to thank team manager Sharpey along with Clak and Podge for all their help and I'd also like to apologise for my numerous strops, huffs and rants thorough out the season. I'd like to apologise to the lads for the 3 points we were deducted at the start of the season.

I'd also like to thank the secretary's from the teams we have played this season ALL have been approachable, honest and friendly no matter what the results have been. All have taking part in Sunday morning football in the passionate, competitive and humorous way it should be.

Is it the end?
No I still intend to help out in running the Villa at a lower level (some habits are hard to kick). Hopefully 2010/2011

145

won't see me have to put my boots on I'm in touching distance of being too old and fat to go with the slow and rubbish that I already was.

Hopefully 2010/2011 will see us promoted in 'the race for the premiership'.

A final word from Steve

Firstly let me thank the management and players of Newcastle United for a wonderful season. It has been so refreshing to see a team that cares pulling on the strip and giving there all for the cause. Thanks to Dawn and Rebecca for their help and support at home and my Mam Celia and in-laws Liz and Jimmy for babysitting duties whilst I attended the games, I'd be lost without you all. Thanks to my Dad and brother Rob for their company at the match and Chris Knowles for the updates via his radio. Thanks to Alan Payne for regular updates on how much he is going to pick up at the bookies after the game and to Dave Beaney and Mike Hall who have kept up their unbeaten records as guests of ours at the match. Thanks to everyone who tuned into 'Toon Talk' this season and everybody who bought 'Players Inc' or attended one of our events. Thanks to Kev for the chance to lift the trophy and a stotting headache after the Ipswich game. Big thanks to Andrew Brewster for designing the cover and Gareth Johnson for proof reading the book. If there is anything wrong with it then it's his fault not mine or Singes.

A final word from Singe

Thanks to Ma and Da for pushing and pushing me as a child to do better in life. I may not have enjoyed it as a bairn and you also said I was the worst writer in class 7.
But I got there in the end with your love and help.
Thanks to Nerise for giving me at times enough rope to hang myself with and for having the patience, strength, time and understanding of a saint.

Everybody at Grange Villa WMC.FC deserves a mention for supplying me the ammunition to fire off some big bombs every Sunday on the Facebook page even though some of them 'are true made up stories' Thanks to my good friends from The Villa youth club for Saturday night fun and a lot of drunken reflections and discussions of the joys of Sunday morning football.

Thanks to The Ultras and the good people from the club for great banter and friendship.

Finally most thanks has to go to Sharpey for giving me 12 wonderful, happy years of his unique brand of football.......I may have been one of your worst footballers but I can honestly say 'I've lived the dream'.